A Rose for

Sergei

K. Kidd

This book is a true story.
Some names have been changed.

Copyright © 2014 by K. Kidd

ISBN-13 978-1502524911
ISBN-10 1502524910

Printed by CreateSpace

This book has been cleared for open publication by the
Department of Defense's Office of Prepublication and
Security Review (DoD/OPSR).

In Memory

of

Sergei Kourdakov

Contents

Prologue

Sergei Kourdakov, a former KGB agent and Soviet naval intelligence officer, defected to Canada more than forty years ago. One of his assignments with the Russian police was to break up secret meetings of Christian "Believers." While serving aboard the surface ship *Elagin,* a Soviet trawler, he jumped overboard when they were near the coast of Canada. His search for freedom began that very day—September 3, 1971. In Canada, he learned to speak English and became a Christian. To say Sergei had a change of heart is an understatement. It would be more accurate to say he found his heart.

In the fall of 1972 Sergei spent several weeks in Washington DC meeting with Government Officials. During that time he met a young secretary with whom he had an instant connection; they were both twenty-one years old. This is their true, bittersweet story...I know because I was that young secretary.

Sergei's book, *The Persecutor*, was not published until after his death. There were many facets about his life that I never knew. Sergei had only told me a shortened version, carefully leaving out parts of his life in the Soviet Union that would have alarmed me if I had known every detail.

I knew the person Sergei had become after he defected. He was honest, smart, gentle, and caring. He was a completely changed person. And that is the person I fell in love with.

Chapter 1

Key Bridge Marriott

Fall 1972

"Excuse me; I would like to go to the men's…how do you say in America…restroom?" Sergei asked in his broken English. "Is that the right way to say that?"

"Yes, that is the right way; you could also say men's room. And it's okay to excuse yourself," I said. "It isn't rude. I'll be fine sitting alone a few minutes at the table until you return," I assured him as I smiled and tried to refrain from laughing. He was so incredibly polite. The way he spoke, his broken English combined with his Russian accent, could be very amusing at times.

We were having dinner at the JW Steakhouse at the Key Bridge Marriott in Arlington, Virginia. My date was Sergei Kourdakov. He was twenty-one years old, and he had defected from the Soviet Union over a year ago. He had been a member of the KGB, the Commissariat for State Security or secret police, and a Soviet naval intelligence officer—intimidating credentials for sure. He was also very good looking, which I found even more intimidating.

I worked as a secretary at the Office of Information for the Armed Forces, a division that came under the Office of the Secretary of Defense. I was also twenty-one years old. We had recently met at my office in Rosslyn, Virginia. Sergei had flown in from Los

1

Angeles and was meeting with Government Officials in Washington DC. Sergei's incredible story was making headlines in the United States. Future plans were being considered for Sergei to record/broadcast his story in another section of our office, the American Forces Radio and Television Service. My boss was the liaison officer tasked with assisting Sergei.

As Sergei got up from the table and sauntered off in search of the men's room, I could see that all eyes in the restaurant were on him. Both men and women stared at him, even the wait staff. I was not surprised at their seemingly awestruck reaction. He was very tall with huge broad shoulders and muscular arms that strained at the seams of his shirt, the result of years of body-building. His stride was confident, purposeful, and he definitely commanded attention. He stood out in any crowd.

While I waited for his return, I leaned back in my chair and enjoyed the view out the windows. The restaurant was on the top floor of the hotel, and you could see all the grandeur of Washington DC, Georgetown, and Georgetown University right across the Potomac River. The view was breathtaking at night with the city lights twinkling ever-so-slightly in the reflection on the water. It was captivating; I never tired of that view. In the early evening the city lights illuminated the streets and radiated a soft, peaceful glow over the city. The lights also helped hide the scary, dark parts of the city, and I liked that.

I wrapped my fingers around the stem of my wine glass just a little too tightly. *It must be a case of "second date nerves,"* I thought. *Just take a deep breath and try to relax*, I told myself. I had been on many dates; however, nothing even came close to this. Sergei was so different from anyone I had ever met, let alone dated. He was a Russian defector whose past history

2

with the KGB was nothing to take lightly. It was serious business, and the element of danger was not lost on me.

My thoughts flashed back to security briefings from when I worked at the Defense Intelligence Agency (DIA). We were taught to be on the lookout for anyone trying to coerce secret information from us. These people could be friends or neighbors, someone that you would not ordinarily suspect. They had a word for people like that...spy. The thought that Sergei could be a spy did cross my mind, but I knew I had never told him I used to work for DIA. I brushed those thoughts away for now since I knew I tended to be overly suspicious sometimes. But then, I always did love mystery and intrigue.

It was hard to believe that Sergei was my date for the evening. When I was a child I was afraid of Russians. I never forgot the air raid drills we had in elementary school. My father was a pilot in the U.S. Air Force and my family lived on military bases. When the air raid siren blasted we practiced hiding under our desks at school, using them for protection from shattered windows, as we prepared for an attack that might one day come from the Soviet Union. And yet, here I was now, having dinner with...the "enemy."

In fact the whole scenario did not seem real, meeting like we did. We were attracted to each other right from the first introduction. That surprised me, not me being attracted to him, but him being attracted to me. Next to Sergei, I thought I seemed rather ordinary—petite, five feet tall, slender, blue-green eyes and long, straight sandy blonde hair that flipped up at the ends. "Cute," is how most people would describe me. Although just recently a DC taxi cab driver told me, "A pretty girl like you should not have to pay for anything!" That taxi ride was definitely one of those scary parts of the city moments.

3

I jumped as I set my wine glass back down on the table. Sergei had quietly returned by way of sneaking up behind me and grabbing my shoulders with both of his hands. His enormous hands seemed to totally engulf my shoulders and upper arms. He had startled me, and he found that rather funny. I looked over my left shoulder and I could see him leaning over me with a huge grin on his face. I had to laugh at myself for being so jumpy. I turned my head back towards the table.

He bent down lower and whispered in my ear, "No, wait."

He then placed one hand at the base of my neck and slowly traced a line with his fingers up my neck. As soon as his fingers reached my chin, he tilted my head upright and straight back so I was looking up toward the ceiling and directly at him as he leaned over me. I was totally entranced; his touch was gentle and cool on my warm skin. It was very sensual, and I felt my heart beating rapidly as I let out a slightly inaudible gasp. I was motionless as he lowered his head and his lips touched mine, ever-so-tenderly. He kissed me several times in this strange, exciting, upside down position, his hand still holding my chin, his fingers caressing my neck, his tongue brushing against my lips. And then suddenly, it was over, and he took his place across the table from me and broke into a huge, satisfied smile.

I sat frozen in my chair. Now that my senses had returned I realized we had created quite a scene right in the middle of the restaurant. Again all eyes were on him and now on me. I hoped people thought my red glow was from embarrassment when in reality my cheeks and neck were hot and flushed from his unexpected display of affection.

"What do you think?" Sergei asked. "Did you like that?"

Did I like that? Was he serious? Did I like that? I was speechless for a minute, trying to compose myself from what was in fact the most incredible kiss I had ever experienced. It was a kiss that renders you powerless because of its intensity and the meaning behind it. And yet it was a gentle, yearning kiss. It was a kiss that exploded through my whole being with a burning desire. It was like fireworks in my mind, my heart, my soul. It was a kiss that you wait for your whole lifetime.

"Ummm...well, yes...I did like that," I shyly responded in all honesty. I prided myself on my honesty but suddenly wished I had demurred on my answer. I was still flushed and self-conscious that the rosy glow on my cheeks lingered and that he could tell how I felt about him. I knew that I was really starting to like him, a lot in fact. I couldn't help but wonder why he asked me if I liked his kiss. I did not have to wait long to find out the reason for his sudden display of affection.

"I kissed you like that because I saw guy kiss girl like that on TV, and I wanted to try it!" he explained in his sexy Russian accent. He had an expression of delight on his face and looked very pleased with himself.

I couldn't help but smile back at him; he had an easy way of making me feel comfortable around him, protected, even with the mind-blowing kiss. How could I be upset about the TV kiss? He looked so proud of himself regarding *that* mission. *Mission accomplished,* I thought. *Very well accomplished and executed indeed.*

We talked incessantly after that, learning more about each other as we enjoyed our dinner. However, I couldn't help but notice that Sergei would periodically look around the restaurant, as if scanning the room for something. *What? What is he looking at, or looking for?* I was curious, but I didn't mention it then. We

5

were having a wonderful time together. And then out of the blue he said the most startling thing to me.

"You are beautiful girl," he said, dragging out the r's in his accent as if saying gurrrl.

His words caught me by surprise, and I blushed slightly. *Well, that comment was certainly unexpected. I could only smile up at him because once again I was speechless.*

"Beautiful girl like you," he said and then hesitated slightly. "Beautiful girl like you…you could be spy!" he said in all seriousness.

He stared at me and through me with his piercing blue eyes, a look of concern…or was it confusion…across his face. My heart sank right then and there.

He thinks I'm a spy! How did I ever end up in a situation like this?

Chapter 2

Major X

Summer 1968

Some of the most popular, sought after jobs for young women in Northern Virginia were secretarial positions with the Federal Government. These positions were exciting and professional—the pay scale was quite good. And it was well known that the health and retirement benefits were better than a lot of private companies. It was secure work; you knew the Federal Government wasn't going to close or move. It was the perfect job after graduating from high school. A college education wasn't always necessary to ensure success in the work place then. If you worked hard and had exceptional typing and shorthand skills then you had an excellent opportunity to move up the ladder—from a secretarial job to an administrative assistant position. And that was just the plan I had in mind.

I knew all of those timed typing tests in high school would pay off eventually. Tests were on a manual typewriter. The keys were covered by placing a sheet of white typing paper over the keyboard, so you were in essence typing blind. My best time was 100 words per minute for a one-minute timed test with no errors. It was an outstanding score. On the other hand, my stenography note-taking skills needed some slight improvement, but I had passing scores.

I landed the perfect summer job in 1968 after a recruiter from DIA came to our business classes at Thomas Jefferson (TJ) High School in Alexandria, Virginia. I was sixteen years old and would soon be finishing my junior year at TJ. Typing, shorthand, English, and business classes were my favorite subjects. It was spring time, and the recruiter was in search of competent students to fill summer clerical positions with DIA. In addition to good business skills, students had to qualify for a security clearance and pass a background investigation with flying colors.

I knew a security clearance would not be a problem. My father was a Lieutenant Colonel in the Air Force and a highly-decorated fighter pilot. He had even set a world flying record in 1954 when he won the Bendix Trophy Race in an F84 Thunderstreak jet. Dad was intelligent and handsome, six feet tall with dark hair and blue eyes. And he loved his family first and foremost. I, along with my three brothers and two sisters, knew how to stay out of trouble. Honesty and respect were just a normal part of growing up on military bases. We were very fortunate to have wonderful and loving parents as role models.

I was thrilled to have obtained an interim clearance, and I started my very first job at a DIA office in Northern Virginia. I was not allowed in certain sections of the building yet, so I had to work in the outer office area only, which was a little confining at times. The office was your typical government office with gray metal desks and gray metal file cabinets. It seemed everything was gray except for the black standard, rotary dial telephones. On the plus side, my supervisor, Mrs. Bradley, and the other secretarial staff were extremely friendly and cheerful. I was fortunate to have such good mentors since my goal was to learn from them, work hard, and be as professional as I could, even though I was the youngest employee at that location. I needed a good recommendation at the end of the summer so that I could apply for a full-time job with DIA after I graduated from high school the following year.

Aside from the all-female secretarial staff, there was a large group of military officers and civilian employees, mostly male, that passed by my outer office area each day en route to their various meetings throughout the rest of the building—classified areas that I was not allowed access to. They were all young, late-twenties to mid-thirties, professional, intelligent, very personable, and extremely polite. They were definitely not like the loud, awkward guys from high school that I was accustomed to seeing. Maybe there was hope for those high school boys later in life when they grew up. I definitely preferred guys that were more mature.

My office duties included typing, copying papers, and filing—lots of filing—organizing papers, answering questions, and directing people to the proper rooms. I was young and inexperienced in the work force, but I was not the least bit uncomfortable speaking with the higher ranking civilians or military officers. Whereas some of the secretarial staff seemed a little in awe of them, I was taught at a very early age to show respect, shake hands, and speak up for myself.

There was always a lot of activity around the office, with people constantly stopping by to ask for forms or help or directions. I was amazed at how busy everyone was.

"What exactly does everyone do in this building?" I asked Mrs. Bradley, the head secretary.

"Most of the people you see each day are attending classes," Mrs. Bradley replied. "This is not their primary work location, they are only here for the summer. When classes are over they will either return to their previous office or be reassigned to a new location overseas."

"Really?" I asked, more curious than ever. That did account for all the comings and goings. "What type of classes are they taking?"

"They are learning different languages and about different cultures. After all, they will be representing our country as an attaché if they take an overseas assignment," Mrs. Bradley responded.

"Sort of like…spies then," I whispered conspiratorially under my breath. I was letting my sixteen-year-old imagination run wild.

"Well no, not like that," Mrs. Bradley laughed. "An attaché is another name for ambassador."

"Oh, okay, now I understand," I replied. I knew about ambassadors, but I was not familiar with the word attaché. That word still sounded spy-like in my mind, and after our discussion, I did look at everyone a little differently. Once when I was filing a stack of papers I saw a group of students pass by, and just for fun I tried to pick out who I thought would make the best spy. One of the civilians caught my eye—it definitely had to be the man with his arm in the black cloth sling, I guessed. He was darkly tanned and had a beautiful head of thick, brown hair. He was quite attractive and had a slight accent. French maybe? He looked very sophisticated, average height and weight. His sport coat did not fit over the cast on his arm so he had to drape his sport coat casually over one shoulder, in a way that gave him a sort of sexy, secretive quality. The way he walked was what caught my attention. He seemed to move about so carefully and effortlessly. In reality I think he was simply trying to keep his sport coat from falling off but the effect was so mysterious. *He probably has a fake cast with all sorts of secret weapons hidden inside,* I thought.

After a few weeks on the job, I met Major X when he stopped by my desk in search of a form he needed. He was in the Air Force and was also taking classes that summer. He was your typical officer type, clean cut, professional, and sharp looking. Major X was one of those rare people who had a great personality and was genuinely nice. He had a kind demeanor, someone you felt like you knew your whole life. People liked him instantly, and so did I. He was in his mid-thirties, had short brown hair, and a carefree smile. He was also very cute.

Most of the people in the summer classes would quickly complete their business in our office and then scurry back to wherever they came from. I was almost invisible to them. Major X, however, would often take a few minutes to ask how I was doing before he went back to class. He found out that my father was an officer in the Air Force and would soon be leaving for a year-long tour of duty in the Vietnam War. He asked about school, my mother, and all my brothers and sisters. He always had a kind word, was sincere, and had a way of brightening each day. He was the type of person that you never forget, and I always looked forward to our brief chats.

As August was coming to an end I was happy to hear from Mrs. Bradley that I was one of the best clerical aides they had ever had and that she would highly recommend me for another position with DIA after I graduated from high school. I was thrilled to hear such positive feedback, and I couldn't wait to share my good news.

When I saw Major X later that day I quickly told him about my conversation with Mrs. Bradley. I was pleased that my hard work was noticed and appreciated and that I had a permanent job lined up for the following year. I also mentioned to him that it was going to be hard going back to school because I enjoyed working and earning my own money.

He congratulated me and assured me that I would quickly readjust to high school. He said he knew that I would have a great senior year. I thanked him for all his kindness towards me and told him how I enjoyed our short daily talks. I knew I would miss him, but I didn't say anything. He was to be a pleasant memory of my first job.

On my last day of work, Major X surprised me when he asked if we could take a walk outside during lunch break. He just wanted a moment to say goodbye, wish me well…and besides, it was a perfect, beautiful, sunny summer day outside.

As we walked along, side-by-side past the building, he talked about my success at my first job. When we reached the end of the block we left the sidewalk to walk up a small, grass covered hill near a bed of bright yellow flowers. It was there by the flowers that his conversation changed to a more personal, serious tone.

"I have something to tell you," he said, pausing slightly before continuing.

At that point he had my complete attention; I had no idea what he wanted to tell me.

"You are going to fall in love more than once in your life before you are married," he softly told me.

I walked along beside him in silence, slightly taken aback. I didn't understand what exactly he was trying to tell me. Did he somehow know that I had a secret schoolgirl crush on him? Had he seen it in my eyes? I had never said anything to make him think that.

He continued speaking in his gentle way. "Let me explain…you might be in love with a man, but if that man loves you and he is not ready for marriage then it will never happen. In other words, the time you will marry is when both of you are in love at the same time and both of you are ready for marriage at the same time. Do you understand? There is not just one person in your life that you will love. There might be several men you will love before you find the one you will marry. Do you understand what I'm saying?"

"Yes, I think so, yes…I do understand," I murmured. I knew he was not referring to the two of us, but I was not sure who he was referring to exactly. He was sincere and intent on telling me this—I knew it was important to him. They were beautiful words that I would always remember. Words that I had no way of knowing at the time would have such an incredible and important relevance in my life.

His "farewell talk" was over, and we turned around to walk back to the office. As we headed down the short hill to the sidewalk one of my high heels got stuck in the dirt, and I started to lose my balance. Major X had already reached the sidewalk. He turned around and offered his hand to steady me. I reached out and our hands entwined briefly as he took a firm grip and gently guided me down the rest of the way. I felt the warmth, strength, and kindness in his strong hand. As soon as I reached the sidewalk he released his grip, flashed a warm smile at me, and we strolled back to work chatting companionably.

When we arrived at the office, we parted ways. He went back to classes, and I went back to the tasks at hand in preparation for leaving my first job. The afternoon flew by quickly. At the end of the day, I thanked the secretarial staff and said my goodbyes. I was gone before Major X completed his afternoon classes.

That was the last time I ever saw Major X.

Chapter 3

Graduation

Summer 1969

Major X was right about one thing—I did enjoy my senior year of high school. TJ was a fairly new school, only five years old at the time I graduated. It wasn't until 1985 that it became the super smart magnet school in Fairfax County. I would later jokingly have to clarify that I went there when it was the "dummy" school. I could joke about it because Fairfax County Public Schools have always been one of the top rated school systems in the nation, and all of their schools provided an excellent education.

I was very anxious to graduate and get back into the working world. A more exciting part of life with unknown adventures was just around the corner, and I could hardly wait. That's not to say I didn't have any exciting high school adventures. Senior year was busy with hours of studying and squeezing in time for fun with friends. But junior year was a different story. I'll definitely never forget the time I went to the infamous "paisley party."

A paisley party is a party where the guys wear their wildest, loudest, paisley print silk boxer shorts under their blue jeans. Later in the evening the girls judge who has the best pair of paisley boxers. Obviously, it was something the guys made up. But it sounded tame enough to me, no different than seeing guys wearing swim trunks. Or so I thought.

But the guys, being young and foolish and…guys, had a different plan. They thought it would be a great joke to strip completely so when we walked in they would all be standing in line, stark naked. And at attention, so to speak. At first glance I thought the guys were holding kielbasa sausages in front of them as a prank. I didn't think they were dumb enough to take all of their clothes off. Then I noticed that their hands and arms were all at ease by their sides. And those definitely were not kielbasas! None of us, neither I, nor any of my girlfriends saw any humor whatsoever in their crazy stunt. The guys ended up profusely apologizing to us the rest of the evening. *After* they put their clothes back on. It was a high school lesson that I never forgot. And I wasn't even taking anatomy classes.

Senior year really did fly by, and graduation was there before I knew it. At the end of the very last day of school I met Jay at my locker to clean out the contents. Jay was my best guy friend, and we shared a locker all during senior year. Just to clarify, he was *not* one of the paisley party gang, and he was dating one of my girlfriends. As we gathered our belongings, one of my notebooks dropped and the three ring clamps opened, spilling dozens of papers all over the floor. When I bent over to pick them up, I did something totally out of character. I let out a huge, loud shriek of joy, picked up the papers, and tossed them wildly up in the air. Jay stood and watched in disbelief. He knew I was usually more reserved. We stood there smiling at each other as we watched the pages flutter and fall all around us. We were really done with high school. Finally! It was exhilarating.

Graduation was exciting but also a little sad because my father was still out of the country and could not join the family celebration. All of my friends would be leaving soon. Most of them were headed off to college, some joined the military of their own accord, and others were called to service via the Vietnam draft lottery. A few of them joined the work force like me. I was about to start working full-time and I was only seventeen years old.

My family graduation party was wonderful thanks to Mom and my brothers and sisters. Mom had the special gift of making each one of us feel unique and loved. She was smart, and pretty with red hair and blue-green eyes. She had a funny sense of humor, which was a necessity when you had such a large family. It was a wonder how she managed everything with Dad gone for the year. Mom was a military wife, and she made it all look so simple: the house, the car, the bills, the cooking, and the piles of laundry—six kids!

I fell right in the middle of everyone, the third child, a middle child. I loved being in the middle. I looked up to my brother Keith, who was four years older than I was. He had also just graduated, from college though, and started his career with the Federal Government. I also looked up to my sister Karen, who was in her second year of college. She seemed a lot wiser even though she was only two years older. She had inherited all of Mom's good qualities.

My younger brothers and sister were always a joy. There was never a lack of fun and games in our home. I loved having such a big family. I felt very fortunate to be surrounded by all their love and acceptance. I treasured each moment at home because I knew changes were just around the corner. The adult world was beckoning me at lightning speed, and I was eager with anticipation.

Chapter 4

The Pentagon

Summer 1969

Just a few days after graduation, I found myself back at work at the Defense Intelligence Agency with not even so much as a summer vacation. I had passed my security background checks and was cleared to work in areas that were classified as Top Secret and above. On my first day, I attended the orientation meeting at the Pentagon along with other new permanent hires. We were receiving our assignments. It turned out that I would be working at another location in Northern Virginia. I was disappointed because I had really wanted to work in the Pentagon. I loved the atmosphere in the Pentagon with all of the hustle and bustle, the importance of it all. I was very patriotic at heart.

I was not the only new employee who wanted to specifically work in the Pentagon. Another young girl had recently graduated from high school and moved from her home in North Carolina with hopes of working in the Pentagon, too. Her name was June. She was seventeen, very cute, and petite like me. She was very vocal about her displeasure when she received her assignment to work at a location outside of the Pentagon, although it was to no avail. I liked her right away with her thick southern accent, and I could tell that she was determined and had spunk. As luck would have it, June and I ended up working in the same office at C Building. Neither of us knew where that was, so we formed our own alliance that day, a friendship that would eventually span decades.

June and I enjoyed our work at C Building—trying to learn all the ropes together. People there thought we were sisters. Her hair was slightly darker than mine, we were exactly the same height and about the same weight, and many had a hard time telling us apart. We became fast friends and found out that we had a lot in common. We had a strong work ethic, a desire to succeed and move up the ladder, and, of course, the same goal to earn more money. One of the well known pitfalls of working in the Northern Virginia area was the high cost of living, and we were starting at the very bottom.

After working only nine months at C Building, I was surprised to find out that I had been selected for a rotational assignment to work on a special project at the Pentagon. The detail was for three months, and then I would return to C Building to my same position. I did not really have a choice, and as June said, at least I would finally be at the Pentagon. My boss and coworkers seemed sure the new office would want to keep me. I, on the other hand, reminded them it was only a three-month assignment and I would return. It turned out they would be right.

Once again, another first day on a new job, and I was eighteen years old. I knew my way around the Pentagon fairly well, but my new temporary office was a little hard to find. It was tucked away in the mezzanine basement of the Pentagon—the basement before the real basement. Who knew there were different levels of basements? I had to ask the Pentagon security guards for directions the first time I reported to work.

There actually was only one small stairwell you could use to get to my new office and that was Stairwell

Number 81. Once you found the mystery stairwell, you had to open the fire door to enter. It was not well lit and too secluded for my comfort. You went down a long flight of stairs to a landing then turned to the right and continued down a second long flight of stairs. When you reached the bottom of the stairs you had to open another door to enter the corridor. Just around the corner was a security guard for the entrance into the DIA section where I was to work. I was glad the security guard was close by because those stairs really gave me the creeps.

My Pentagon assignment was amazing. I had been selected to be an editorial assistant for a top secret intelligence report called the Crisis Situation Alert Report. It was a monthly report, about ten-twelve pages long, and I was the sole typist in charge of the entire design layout. My secretarial skills were excellent, but I had no experience with design and layout whatsoever. After a little instruction it turned out I was a natural, and I found that I loved that type of work. I used the latest IBM Selectric typewriter along with different element "balls" for font changes, correction tape (a typist's best friend), and an exacto knife to trim the photos. Next to my desk was a special work table with a grid and a light underneath to align the photos on the pages. There was no room for mistakes; the report contained all of the major crises around the world. Another part of my job was to make sure it was error free and camera ready before it was sent to be printed. I was a detail-oriented person, which is the reason, I was sure, that I was selected for the assignment. The editor of the publication was an excellent tutor. He was a perfectionist and nothing ever slipped by him.

It turned out that the report had quite a large distribution list in the intelligence world. Even my brother Keith, who worked at *the other agency—the*

Central Intelligence Agency—received a copy. That was the hardest part about the type of work I did—I could never tell anyone exactly *what* I did. I was as vague as possible when I told Keith I typed a monthly crisis report and placed pictures in it, but he knew what I was referring to. The pictures I "stuck in" were actually Top Secret photos of tanks, missiles (Inter-Continental Ballistic Missiles), and other military weapons.

On month three of my detail I found out that I would be preparing the final issue of the report. The report had been phased out, and the new office would be reorganized with the need for a full-time secretary with strong office skills. I was offered the new position and quickly accepted the job. I would be staying with DIA in the Pentagon, in the mezzanine basement. A much-welcomed promotion soon followed.

It was fascinating work. I particularly remember the first time I was asked to assist our head office with a critical typing project that required a security clearance above Top Secret, which I now held. It was highly sensitive, a "need-to-know" or "eyes only" document. I was required to type the papers in a vault/room with an armed guard at the door. I was more than just a little nervous with the guard standing by watching and I had to start over a number of times. I think the guard actually cringed each time I spotted a typo and ripped the paper from the typewriter carriage, with the tell-tale, rapid-fire *click, click, click, click* sound echoing in the empty space. I hoped he set the safety catch on his gun. I had done more than my share of filling up the red and white striped burn bag beside the desk.

Finally, when everything was typed to perfection, I carefully stamped the words "Top Secret" at the top and bottom of each page. The higher classification of this document required another security stamp, which was also secured in the vault. This was the first time I ever had to use a code word stamp on a document, and it was hard to keep my hands from trembling as I positioned the rubber stamp at the bottom of each page. *Oh my God, I can't believe what I just typed, and I can't tell anyone!* When I returned to my office everyone was waiting to hear what I thought about working in the vault. "Well…that was interesting," was all I could tell them. I think my eyes were as wide as saucers. They all smiled; they knew that was the only information I could divulge. It was a "type it and forget about it" project. I learned at a very young age how to keep a secret.

As much as I enjoyed my time at the Pentagon I was more than ready to work in a building where you could see the sunshine each day—working in the mezzanine basement of the Pentagon left a lot to be desired. You never knew if it was day or night because you couldn't see the sun. The mice liked to run around down there, too. It was a good thing I wasn't afraid of them. I laughed about that because the DIA officers in my room warned me that if I ever arrived first at work, I shouldn't just walk right in. I needed to open the door, reach my arm in to turn on the lights, and then bang on the wall to scare all of the mice away. Yes, there were plenty of mice in the basement.

I had read somewhere that there were still people who truly believed that aliens from another planet were kept in the basement of the Pentagon for scientific experiments. I can positively say that aliens were not kept in the basement of the Pentagon. One day I delivered some papers to an office in the basement with a coworker. "Shhhh…do you see any aliens down here?" I quietly quipped.

"No waaay," was the reply. It was hard to contain our laughter.

* * *

21

I was right about the scary stairwell to the mezzanine basement though. I was followed one day on my way back from the concourse area after lunch. I had opened the door to the stairwell and I was only a few steps down the first flight of stairs when I heard the door behind me open again. The sound of heavy, running feet sent an alarming tingle through my body, and I felt the hair stand up on the back of my neck. It was a sensation I had never experienced. I started running, taking some stairs two at a time in my high heels to get away.

I heard the pounding sound of footsteps closing in on me so I jumped the last three stairs to the bottom landing to quickly reach the safety of the door at the bottom of the stairs. I knew the security guard was right outside that door, but I had to stop in order to pull the door inwards. I screamed and tried to pull on the door as the stranger slipped his arm around my waist and pulled me back against him. My scream was enough to send him running back up the stairs in the other direction. I was only slightly rattled since I knew help was so close at hand. I didn't think things like that could happen in a secure building. I had spotted his security clearance badges hanging around his neck when I swung around to push against his shoulders.

I filed a report with Pentagon Security, but the man was never found. Thankfully, everyone took it very seriously. I was issued a Joint Chiefs of Staff security badge for the sole purpose of cutting through their corridor. The badge allowed me to access a private metal circular set of stairs that connected the Joint Chiefs of Staff offices and the Defense Intelligence Agency offices. You could not enter that area without proper identification. It was a safe resolution to the problem.

* * *

It had been one year since my last promotion and I was now eligible to move up a pay grade. I knew my current job didn't support a higher grade though. That meant, if I wanted to move up, I would have to change offices. I had heard about a new job that just opened up, but that would mean leaving the Defense Intelligence Agency and the Pentagon. The position I applied for was with the Office of Information for the Armed Forces, a division which came under the Office of the Secretary of Defense (OSD). The new job would be in Rosslyn, Virginia, which was only a short three-mile commute from the Pentagon. I heard from my friends that OSD had more opportunities for moving up in the secretarial field. I was ready for a change and a much-needed promotion. I interviewed and a few weeks later I was hired for the new job in Rosslyn. I couldn't believe my good fortune.

Chapter 5

Rosslyn

Winter 1971

I don't know what I was happier about, the promotion or a chance to work in a building where I could tell if it was day or night or snowing or raining. I had windows and sunshine. My new office was located on the fourth floor of the Pomponio Building in Rosslyn, Virginia. The reception area where my desk was situated had a wall of windows at the end of the room. I had a view to die for that overlooked the Key Bridge and Georgetown.

My pay raise could not have come at a better time because I was basically on my own now. When my father returned from the Vietnam War he received his orders for his next assignment to an Air Force base in Massachusetts, and my family had recently moved there. One of the most difficult decisions I ever had to make was to stay and continue working in the DC area and watch my family move without me. The reason my parents relented to my staying was because my brother Keith was living nearby should any emergency come up.

I missed my family terribly. It was hard not to see my mom and dad, brothers, and sisters on a daily basis. Even my older sister, Karen, left with the family to finish college in Massachusetts. Without a doubt I would miss her. I would also miss the half of my wardrobe that went with her. We often shared clothes, sometimes willingly and sometimes not so willingly. It depended on who got home first and could raid the closet before their date arrived. She often half-heartedly joked that her clothes went out on more dates than she did and probably had more fun. She was right, but I didn't let her know that. The good news was that she was engaged and would eventually return to live in the area after her wedding. I especially missed my mother and her hugs, advice, strength, and most of all her friendship. I knew it would be a hard adjustment to make without all of my family for support.

Thank goodness for June and our alliance. She was a true best friend. As soon as she heard my father was being transferred, she invited me to live with her family in their large, spacious apartment in Alexandria. It was hard for all of us to try to make ends meet and having one more person to share the rent would benefit everyone.

I quickly fit right in with June and her mother Bertie Mae, younger sister Susan, and her cousin Alice. They were wonderful to me, and soon became my second family. Bertie Mae was soft spoken, pretty, and petite. Her special "chili soup" nights always reminded me of home. Alice was kind and sweet natured. She spent long hours at work and was frequently gone. Susan was twelve, cute, and had an impish nature…she loved to tease June. I became the middle sister again, often intervening in Susan's sisterly pranks. Surprisingly, for five women living under the same roof and sharing bathrooms and kitchen space, we managed quite well without ever having any difficulties.

I enjoyed the people I worked for at the Office of Information for the Armed Forces, both military personnel and civilians. It was in this office that I received my first-ever nickname. It was the result of a slight misunderstanding between a new Army Major and me. After a few weeks he still had a hard time remembering my name and when he did, he always mispronounced it. One day after numerous times of trying to correct him I finally exasperatedly said, "If you can't pronounce my name right, then just don't say it at all." He definitely took offense, and I felt horrible. My statement had not come out at all how I intended. I just felt that if we were going to work together he could at least remember my name and pronounce it correctly. His face started to redden as he tried to maintain his composure.

"Well, then, all right...*SAM*," he said as he glared back at me.

The thought of me being called Sam, just plain Sam, broke the tension between us as we doubled over into shared laughter. After that I was known as Sam to everyone in the office. I really enjoyed working for Major Ronald and had the utmost respect for him after the slight misunderstanding.

I shared the secretarial duties with Millie, who was close to retiring. Even with the vast age difference we worked well together. We were considered to be part of a secretarial pool. Additionally we were each assigned to be a primary secretary to one of the two top-ranking supervisors in the office.

I was assigned to the ever indomitable and stubborn Mr. Kirk H. Logie. Sr., the Special Assistant for Executive Liaison. He was a high-ranking civilian, at the top of the GS pay scale, and his notorious behavior was often commensurate with his GS status. He was from New Zealand, middle-aged and attractive for a man of his age, with a full head of wavy red hair and a temper to match. And I absolutely adored him. I had been told that his last two secretaries were often in tears and had left because of him; he just couldn't seem to keep a secretary. That is…until I came along. I don't know what it was, but we hit it off right from the start. If he needed something done yesterday, I had already done it yesterday. I was efficient, and he appreciated that. I was sure my military upbringing was a plus, too, as I could stand up to him, all five feet of me.

I was determined to not let him get to me like the other secretaries, and my plan seemed to have worked. After only a short time there I met Mr. Logie's wife. Beverley was also from New Zealand and quite pretty with a very kind and warm personality. They had five adopted children, and their love for each other and their family was always apparent. Before you knew it, Mr. Logie and I fell into an easy working relationship based on respect, trust, and friendship.

The type of work I was doing at my new office dealt with public relations, and I enjoyed the change from the secrecy of the intelligence world. The American Forces Radio and Television Service (AFRTS) side of our office always had interesting people in the building to do stories or interviews. I never knew who I was going to be speaking with or meeting. Mr. Logie always introduced me to the special guests, and I was fortunate to meet and talk with Mel Blanc (the voice of Bugs Bunny) and Leif Erickson, who played Big John Cannon on the television series *High Chaparral*. The nicest and friendliest person I ever spoke with on the phone was Bill Daily, who played Major Healey on the *I Dream of Jeannie* show. It's a wonder that man didn't yell or hang up on me after I called him in California and woke him up after forgetting the time difference on the west coast. He was quite charming! This job definitely had some advantages; it was always interesting and I could tell my friends about my work. Mr. Logie always made sure things were as interesting as possible.

Once again I told myself how fortunate I was to work there. I had made several new friends with the AFRTS staff. Ellen was the secretary, and she was simply amazing. She was a Marine warrant officer's wife and the most gung ho, cutest little ball of fire you have ever seen. Ralph, a very tall, nice-looking radioman in the Navy was a no nonsense tell-it-like-it-is guy and yet had the kindest heart in the world. And then there was tough-guy Dale who had been to Vietnam a few times. He had to be the poster boy as the epitome of a Marine soldier—always polished, attractive, and picture-perfect—but I knew he had a gentle side also.

One morning Mr. Logie walked past my desk and called out in a voice loud enough for everyone in the office to hear, "Sam, I'm sorry. I'm sorry for what I did."

"Why? What happened? What did you do?" I thought he had hit my car in the underground parking garage. He knew how much I loved my dark green 1970 fastback Mustang.

"I'm sorry; I need to apologize to you. I did a terrible thing," he repeated quickly in his New Zealand accent.

Now he had everyone's interest, and our coworkers came out of their offices to find out what happened. I kept waiting to hear bad news about my car, holding my breath just a little.

"Sam, I missed a meeting that I forgot to put on my calendar. I was embarrassed and didn't know what to say so I told them that you forgot to put it on my calendar," he mumbled and fumbled about as his face turned the color of his red hair.

"You did what?" I responded, in shock. "You told them *I forgot* about your meeting?"

"I'm sorry, I know you would never forget an appointment, but I forgot to tell you and I missed it. I feel terrible that I blamed it on you," he confessed for all to hear. That day went down as a red letter day. Mr. Logie actually apologized...and in public. He was doing his best at damage control in case the story came back to haunt him. I just shook my head, smiled, and asked him to please not do that again. Our working relationship would stay on good ground for a long, long time. I really did enjoy working for him. You never knew what to expect.

Chapter 6

"Meet Sergei"

Fall 1972

Fall is my absolute favorite time of year and not just because my birthday is in September. I always associated it with the beginning of a new year, probably left over from school days. It always symbolized a fresh start. And a fresh start is exactly what I needed in the fall of 1972.

As I was sitting at my desk working on my latest assignment, Mr. Logie asked me if I would place a call to Stuttgart, Germany via the military patch office in the Pentagon. No one in the office had better luck putting calls through to overseas areas than I did. They could never understand why the military patch personnel always put my calls through first and so fast.

Our director, an Army Colonel, would get so frustrated when he would have to wait and wait for his overseas calls to go through. I often heard the sound of his phone hitting the cradle as he slammed it down and hollered out, "This shouldn't have to take so long. And I'm a full Colonel." Who was I to tell him that common courtesy and politeness went a long way, something the higher-ups sometimes overlooked when they were in the middle of a crisis situation that demanded immediate attention? Maybe it helped that I was a young female with a very pleasant telephone voice, hmmm, just maybe.

After I successfully placed the call to Germany for Mr. Logie in record time, my mind drifted. Germany was so far away, but my memories of someone very near and dear to me transferring there were not.

It had been more than a year since I last saw Jim. I remembered his boyish good looks and the smile that never left his face. We had maintained a long-distance relationship for over a year while he attended West Point. I missed him when we were apart, and I knew he missed me, too. I thought about the way he would always hold doors open for me wherever we went, and when I would thank him he always responded with "my pleasure." Once when I gave him a questioning look he explained, "Hey, what can I say, I'm an officer and a gentleman." He was definitely right about that.

I had hoped when Jim graduated that we would be able to be together more and see where things were leading. I was with him for his special day when he graduated from West Point. That evening, after graduation and the formal dance were over, we took a ride in his beautiful new, bright canary yellow, Porsche 914. We parked on a bridge to take one last look at the surrounding area before he had to pack up and leave the next day.

Alone at last, we finally embraced and kissed passionately under the starlit night. It was there that Jim told me he received his assignment to go to Germany, and he could not take me with him. He was beginning a whole new chapter in his life and did not even know himself what was in store. In my heart of hearts I knew he was right, but his words stung. The Porsche would go to Germany and I would stay.

I was not angry with him; promises were never made. We stood there for a while longer on the bridge, my back against his chest, his arms wrapped tightly around my waist. I would not forget this night. And in that quiet moment, a memory from a few years before floated through my mind. At that very second I knew exactly what Major X had tried to explain to me...the time was not right. Love was not enough. *Major X, you were right. How did you know?*

My thoughts were suddenly interrupted. Mr. Logie had completed his phone call and stopped by my desk to go over his schedule with me. "Sam, I have a short meeting downstairs with AFRTS. From there I'm going directly to the Pentagon." I was amazed at the amount of work Mr. Logie accomplished. Everything was black or white where he was concerned—he got to the point quickly, and took care of business. "And when I return, I'm going to bring Sergei Kourdakov back with me. He's the young Russian defector I told you about. Sergei's a wonderful young man, he's very interesting. I think you would really enjoy meeting him." *Hmmm...I would enjoy meeting a Russian defector*, I thought. As Mr. Logie rushed off to his meetings, he turned and called back over his shoulder, "Oh and I think Sergei's about the same age as you." I detected a slight smile on his face. *What is he up to now?*

I would find out soon enough. When Mr. Logie returned to our office a few hours later, I looked up from my typewriter and watched him slowly stroll in with Sergei, just as he promised. They headed straight for my desk.

"Meet Sergei," Mr. Logie said in a rather loud, resounding voice.

I glared at Mr. Logie as they stood before me—Mr. Logie with bright, twinkling eyes, and Sergei with a huge smile on his face. Sergei towered over him and was built like a gladiator or a Greek God or...I didn't know what at that moment. I could barely speak as

Mr. Logie stood there with a smug look, like he had just swallowed a canary. At that moment I wanted nothing other than to strangle my boss because I hadn't even combed my hair or applied fresh lip gloss since lunch time.

"Sergei, this is my wonderful secretary, Sam," Mr. Logie proudly said.

"Hello, it is nice to meet you," Sergei responded in his thick Russian accent.

I stood up from my desk to say hello and shake his hand. I felt so small in his presence, and I had to lean my head far back just to be able to look up into his face. As I stood, Sergei took my hand, shook it, and then continued to hold onto it. I noticed that his hands were more than twice the size of my own.

"You have very small hands," Sergei said as he examined my fingers.

Now that I was standing, I realized even with heels on, that I only came to the middle of his chest. In an instant both of his hands were holding my hand as he gently turned it over studying it. *He must not have ever seen dainty hands before.* I was starting to feel a little embarrassed as Mr. Logie stood by watching quietly at attention, still smiling with his hands folded in front of him at waist level.

"It's nice to meet you, too," I finally murmured as I gently pulled my hand back.

"But, Sam is boy's name. You are not boy," he replied as he stared down at my mini-skirt. He had a slightly confused smile on his face as he spoke, "I do not understand."

"You are right, I'm not a boy," I replied as I laughed softly at his conclusive remark. "Sam is my nickname. I'm called Sam because *some* people have trouble pronouncing my real name." My first name had an unusual spelling so I started to spell it for him. "My name starts with a K," I said.

"Oh, so your name is K," he proudly announced before I could finish spelling it.

I smiled at him, "You can call me Sam or just K, whichever is easier." He said he would like to call me K.

Mr. Logie went on to explain about Sergei's meetings in Washington DC, telling me that Sergei now lived in Los Angeles and would be visiting our offices again over the next few months. With that explanation, he took Sergei and left to walk around the office to introduce him to the other staff members.

Whew, well that was an interesting meeting, funny how Sergei kept hold of my hand. Maybe that's just the way Russians like to shake hands, a very warm greeting. I certainly felt a little warm after that, but I told myself to brush those feelings away and concentrate on my work. I wanted to finish my project before the end of the day. Besides, it was Friday, and I was looking forward to some time off. I didn't have any particular plans for the weekend, but I needed time to catch up on things around my apartment.

I had recently moved to Arlington to my own apartment. The move was a huge leap of faith on my part, largely because of the extra expenses I would incur. It would also be the first time in my twenty-one years that I lived alone—no more roommates. I welcomed the change, but in the beginning it was hard to get used to the quiet. I missed living with June and her family and all of the fun, noise, and chaos we had over the past few years.

After Mr. Logie and Sergei had made the rounds through our department they retreated to Mr. Logie's office. Within a few minutes my intercom rang. It was Mr. Logie asking me to come into his office because he had something to discuss. I couldn't imagine what he had in mind since Sergei was still with him.

"What can I help you with?" I asked as I smiled at both of them. Sergei was seated in a chair and stood and smiled when I entered the room. It was hard not to stare at him; he was very charming.

"Sam, I need to take Sergei shopping to help him find an overcoat. It's colder here than in Los Angeles this time of year. Sergei was not prepared for this kind of weather, and he's going to need a coat this weekend. I noticed that you have a nice trench coat, and I wondered where you found it," Mr. Logie explained.

"Oh sure, yes, I just bought my trench coat and I love it." Tan trench coats were extremely popular and in-demand that season. I always tried to keep up with the latest fashion trends. "My coat has a zip-out wool lining so you can wear it year-round. It took me a long time to find it. I looked in all of the department stores at Landmark Center, and I finally found it at Sears—who would have thought to look there? It's very well made, and I got it for a great price."

"Great, we should all make a run to Sears. There's one just down the road," Mr. Logie informed me.

"We," I repeated, surprised by this sudden plan of his. Secretly, I did want to get to know Sergei a little better. I tried not to look overly excited and was very casual about it.

"Yes, we'll need your help to pick out a coat; it shouldn't take long. We'll be back before you know it! Let's go, grab your things. I'll drive."

I had my orders, and besides, it sounded like fun. As the three of us left the office, Mr. Logie shouted goodbye to everyone and informed them we would be back shortly. There were a lot of puzzled looks. It was highly unusual for him to leave work to run an errand, but he didn't say exactly where or what we were up to either. It seemed so clandestine, a secret adventure in the middle of the work day, and a great way to spend a Friday afternoon at work.

We took the elevator to the basement and headed towards Mr. Logie's new maroon Mustang. He had recently purchased it after I had given him a ride to the Pentagon in my Mustang when he missed the Department of Defense shuttle bus. I offered to sit in the back seat since I knew there was very little leg room in the back of Mustangs. I could scoot in and out without a problem. I knew there was no way that Sergei was ever going to fit in the back seat comfortably unless he bent over and curled himself into a pretzel or hung his legs out of the window. Sergei, however, still insisted that I sit up front. I was not surprised by his display of good manners. I watched as he tried to maneuver his large frame to fit himself in the back seat. I refrained from laughing though because he was making a genuine effort to be a gentleman.

"You are not going to fit in the back seat," I finally told him. As he tried once more to squeeze himself in I grabbed his arm to pull him back out. I literally had to fight Sergei for the back seat of the car. He burst into laughter at the sight of me trying to pull him out of the car. He loved the attention and played along as if I had super strength. He pretended to fly out of the back seat and stumbled across a few empty parking spots commenting on how strong I was.

"Really, just sit in the front seat where you will fit," I admonished with a slight smile. "It's okay for me to sit in the back seat of the car."

"Yes ma'am!" he shouted in his best English as he tried not to laugh. He stood at attention, clicked his heels together loudly and saluted me.

Mr. Logie looked at both of us, patiently waiting for the two little kids to stop fighting for a seat in the car.

Oh this is so embarrassing...both of us acting like children in front of my boss. Since I won, I stepped into the back seat as graciously as I could. As I did, I couldn't help but wonder about Sergei. He certainly didn't act like he had been a member of the KGB. He was so good-natured and played along with letting me have my way. I was trying to be polite, and I know he was, too. To me he acted like a big happy kid, sort of like my brother would act. But not like my older brother, not even like my middle brother; he acted like my baby brother. One thing I did notice was that Sergei enjoyed being treated like a normal person. I had the feeling that it was something he did not get to experience too often...if ever.

I didn't realize what a strange group we were until we reached the store and made our way towards the men's overcoat section. There was the red headed, professional-looking older man with his quirky fast New Zealand accent. Then there was the tall, ruggedly handsome young man with huge broad shoulders who spoke broken English in a thick Russian accent. And finally there was me, the petite, slight of build, young blonde female, who spoke perfect English and seemed to be somewhat bossy. We were an odd trio indeed, and we made quite a comedic scene at the store. I don't think Sergei was used to having someone like me help him select his clothes. And I wasn't at all used to running an errand like this with my boss. Sergei looked like he was the kind of guy that was used to calling all of the shots, and here I was taking charge, handing him coat after coat, "Here, try this on. No, I don't like that on you, try this other one on."

As I stood holding Sergei's sport coat, he would try on each trench coat then check the fit in the mirror. "You really should be wearing your sport coat while you're trying on overcoats," I suggested. "You want to make sure you have enough room in the shoulders and that you can move your arms comfortably." I casually handed Sergei back his sport coat and then smiled to myself because I got to check him out in the mirror each time he tried on a new coat. It was so out of character for me, but I couldn't keep from staring. For some reason I was drawn to him. *I really do have the best job in the world.*

It was hard to find a coat to fit because his shoulders and biceps were enormous, but Mr. Logie was determined we would find one. Sergei enjoyed all of the attention. He was laughing and smiling, playfully showing off in the mirror, and I thought to myself...*he has quite a fun-loving personality.* After a lot of effort we finally found the perfect trench coat. It was tan with shoulder and cuff epaulets, the decorative flaps that button down for added detail. It had an inverted pleat in the back and a matching belt that you could tie or buckle. And it looked great on him.

"There, that's the one. I like that one on you, Sergei. It fits and it looks really nice on you."

"Yes, I like this coat," replied Sergei. He was checking out how he looked in the mirror, turning from front to back. A big smile crossed his face; the cut suited his build perfectly. He looked very striking and professional. Sergei reached up to the collar of the trench coat and slowly turned it upwards toward his face. He then tucked both hands in the pockets and pretended to look around cautiously. "I look like spy," he joked. Then he looked directly at me, leaned over and whispered, "I look okay?"

"Yes, you look very okay," I said as I smiled back at him. Sergei then pulled me over close to his side so he could see both of our reflections in the store mirror. He commented that we looked good together...in our matching tan trench coats. He placed his arm across my shoulders and continued to stare into the mirror at me, at us. I was caught up in his gaze and could not take my eyes away from the mirror image of him. I couldn't have agreed more, but I just stood next to him and smiled. Mr. Logie watched us, taking everything in with a big smile on his face. When Sergei took the coat off, Mr. Logie leaned over to me and quietly told me that he would purchase it for him since Sergei was traveling and was a little short on funds. That was just like Mr. Logie to do that, and it did not surprise me.

We quickly headed to the check out area only to find a rather long line of people. We would be waiting a while before it was our turn since we were quite far back, and the line was not moving at all.

As we stood in line Sergei leaned against a column that had a metal bar protector wrapped all around the bottom; the bar was about a foot off the ground. He turned sideways and decided to prop his foot up on the metal bar. I know he must have been tired from his long trip from the west coast, and we were not about to move forward in line anytime soon. I was standing right next to him when he suddenly leaned over, placed both of his hands around my waist, and effortlessly picked me up like I weighed nothing.

"Aahhh…," I couldn't help but let out a small yell of surprise as he placed me on his thigh, which had formed a type of make-shift bench with his leg propped up on the column.

"What are you doing? Put me down, please put me down," I tried to tell him quietly as everyone in line turned to see what all the noise and commotion was about. Everyone was watching us, and I was mortified. He held me firmly in place, his hands on my waist for support, forcing me to remain seated while both of my feet dangled a foot off the ground. Mr. Logie stood there doing his best not to laugh out loud at my precarious situation. He was totally enjoying the spectacle and nodded slightly at me as if to say, "Hey, I'm not getting involved in this."

"Sergei, you have to put me down now," I said in a stern but quiet voice as everyone continued to stare at us. He acted as if this was a very normal thing to do, me sitting on his leg-bench in the middle of a store, just waiting in line.

"No, it is okay," he said determinedly, loud enough for everyone around us to hear, his Russian accent very apparent. "Beautiful girl like you should not have to stand."

The shoppers, along with Mr. Logie, just smiled and chuckled at my predicament while I sat on Sergei's leg. I hoped the fact that Sergei was obviously a foreigner and new to this country might explain his overly expressive and unusual actions. *How professional does this look?*

I looked up at Sergei as he stood there nonchalantly with a very satisfied smile on his face. I knew I wasn't going to win this time, so I resolved to just smile and sit on top of his leg while trying to preserve as much dignity as possible. It was the least I could do. After all, he did say he thought I was beautiful...and in front of my boss and a whole lot of strangers.

Chapter 7

The Desk

Fall 1972

The impromptu shopping spree and the ride back to the office were over sooner than I had hoped. Sergei and I laughed and talked easily in the car while Mr. Logie drove and occasionally chimed in with questions about Sergei's new life in the U.S.

When we arrived at the office parking garage, Sergei offered me his hand to help me out of the back seat of the car. I didn't know if it was intentional or not but when he took my hand, he pulled so hard that I flew out of the back seat and stumbled into his waiting arms. I clung onto him and wrapped my arms around his waist for support as I regained my footing. I looked up at him, our bodies pressed tight against each other, and his slight smile hinted that he definitely enjoyed my unintentional bear hug. I didn't mind in the least either. Before he released me, Sergei reached out and gently brushed back a section of my hair that spilled across my face when I fell forward. Without a doubt the surprise attraction we both felt for each other was strong and obvious.

As we walked toward the elevator he nonchalantly draped his arm over my shoulders, pulling me closer to his side in a protective cocoon-like fashion, and thanked us for helping him find his coat. I could feel his strength and warmth along the entire side of my body, and I liked the easy comfort of him. I liked him plain and simple, and I could not even explain why. We broke apart when the elevator arrived, and the three of us rode up still laughing about the shopping trip until we reached the fourth floor. When we arrived at our office, I reluctantly settled in at my desk in the reception area while Sergei and Mr. Logie went directly to his office.

What an amazing afternoon. I was sure it would be only a one-time adventure with Sergei and then he would return to Los Angeles and I would never see him again. I know I had enjoyed myself, and Sergei seemed to be genuinely having a good time. He was friendly and easy going, and I could not sense any pretense on his part at all. I wanted to get to know him better. Even though I was embarrassed in the store when he picked me up, I had to admit that I loved being held in his huge strong arms.

Now that I was back at my desk, I retrieved my papers from the side drawer where I had quickly tossed them when we left unexpectedly. Trying to get myself reorganized, I spread a few pages across my desk to see where I had left off on my work. I still wanted to finish before the end of the day. I was back on track and busily typing away when suddenly Sergei appeared in front of me.

"Hello K, I would like to talk to you," Sergei said quietly, not wanting the others in the office to hear him. As he stood there, he reached down and carefully started moving objects away from the center front area of my desk. He slid my name plate over, followed by my desk pen set, and then he picked up the papers I had just spread out and neatly stacked them to the side along with the other objects. When he was done, he sat on the front edge of my desk with one leg hanging over the side and one leg still on the ground. He made himself right at home, totally unaware of how out of place he looked in our office.

"What are you doing?" I whispered. "You can't sit on my desk out here in the open like this. Someone might come into our office."

"I want to talk to you," he repeated.

"All right, but you can't sit on my desk. You need to get off," I responded indignantly.

"I would like for you to go out with me on Saturday," he whispered as he leaned across the desk, closer to me.

"Sergei, can you please get off of my desk before I get into trouble?" I pleaded even though I was totally captivated by his good looks.

"Well, tell me you will go out with me and then I will get off of your desk," he replied with a pleased look on his face.

"Yes. Yes, I'll go out with you," I replied, not quite believing he asked me out so soon.

"Good, please write down your telephone number, and I will call tonight to make plans."

I tore off a small sheet of paper from my note pad, wrote down my address and phone number and handed it to him. I watched as he filed the paper in his wallet for safekeeping. He smiled and slowly got up from my desk, carefully moving everything back into place before he headed back to see Mr. Logie. It was 5:00, time to go home. My project would have to wait until Monday, and I didn't even care. Sergei would be calling me soon to make plans. I loved listening to him talk in his Russian accent.

My heart started to beat a little faster as I stood waiting for the elevator. I couldn't wait to see Sergei and learn all about the mysterious life he had left behind.

He was fascinating, even with the little I knew about him. It was going to be a very interesting weekend after all.

Chapter 8

As Seen on TV

Fall 1972

Saturday morning I was up early. I had a hard time sleeping and tossed and turned during the night. I was looking forward to spending the afternoon with Sergei. I showered leisurely and washed and set my long hair with large brush rollers. It would take about forty-five minutes to dry under my hair dryer, and I wanted my hair to be clean and shiny so the leftover highlights from summer would be noticeable. I could tell Sergei liked my long hair. He had offhandedly brushed it back from my face the day before when he helped me out of the car. I was touched by that tender gesture; it seemed out of character for a former KGB agent.

I dressed in a casual outfit, black slacks and a new dark green pullover sweater. It was perfect for a fall afternoon, and it flattered my figure. I felt like I was in high school again—my stomach was actually flip flopping, and I felt a little giddy. It was strange for me to be affected like that by someone so quickly, but he was not your typical someone. He was surrounded by mystery.

Sergei needed a few new shirts for upcoming meetings in DC with government officials and asked if I would join him for another shopping trip that afternoon. I was sure he liked my fashion sense, and we did have a very entertaining shopping trip searching for his coat the day before. It would be an enjoyable date, no pressure, and we could spend time getting to know each other. He told me he was staying in Washington DC as a guest at the Christian Fellowship House and he would catch a taxi to my apartment in Arlington.

Even though I had recently moved into my apartment, it was quite organized—primarily because I did not have much furniture. I did have a lot of clothes, shoes, and handbags though, so I was glad my apartment had several large closets. I was a firm believer in the adage, "Dress for the job you want, not for the job you have." I liked to look professional in the office.

I had a fairly new wood bedroom set thanks to June's cousin Alice, who offered it to me at a very reasonable price when I moved out. It was practically a gift, and I was overwhelmed by her kindness. At least I had a place to sleep at night, if nothing else.

My used sofa, compliments of Ralph from AFRTS, was exactly what I needed. He couldn't believe there wasn't a place to even sit down in my own living room. Inexpensive end tables sat on either side of the sofa and my sewing machine cabinet did double duty as a TV stand. The small black and white TV atop it was sold to me by Mr. Logie.

I was able to pick up two new table lamps with the S&H green stamp books that my mother sent me. She collected green stamps each time she shopped at certain supermarkets or gas stations. The stamps were a marketing incentive to keep customers coming back, and were easily redeemed for merchandise at an S&H redemption center. That was a good thing since I had overextended my budget when I purchased a new kitchen table and chairs. Everything in my apartment was simple and practical. All in all, it was home to me, and I was proud. I was finally on my own.

When Sergei arrived, I met him at the door and was immediately taken aback. He stood there with a heartwarming smile on his face and was so excited that he leaned right over and gave me a huge hug. I was almost lost in his arms as he wrapped them around me and held me in a warm embrace. I loved his greeting; he didn't have any reservations about letting me know how he felt.

"K, I am happy you could go with me today, it is very good," Sergei told me.

"Yes, it is very good. I'm happy too," I replied with a slight smile as I mimicked his English. I was elated, but I tried to be a little more reserved and not seem too eager. He was so gregarious in all of his actions and not afraid to show or tell his true feelings like most guys were. It was a refreshing change and something that I could easily get used to. He stepped inside and immediately started checking out my apartment.

"This is your apartment, you live alone?" he asked. "Is it okay to see apartment?"

"Yes, I live alone, and yes you can take a look around." I smiled as I watched him. It was a funny question to ask the minute he walked in the door, but I thought he was just curious to see how Americans lived.

He seemed satisfied after he made his quick walk through and looked in all of the closets. As soon as he was done scoping out the place he turned and smiled, "Let's go."

We were excited to get started on our shopping trip, so we headed right out to my car. I handed him the keys to my Mustang and asked if he wanted to drive, which was a big thing to me since I never let anyone drive my car. I didn't think he was the type of guy who wanted to be a passenger in a car driven by a female. He declined and settled right in, leaning his bucket seat way back to enjoy the ride.

As soon as we pulled away from the curb I asked
Sergei if he minded stopping by to meet my sister and
her husband. I told him that we would be driving right
past their apartment anyway. I glanced sideways in the
car; just in time to catch Sergei's surprised reaction
about meeting my sister so soon. Sergei's response to
my question was touching. I noticed the slight gleam in
his bright eyes as he broke into a huge smile, "This is
not problem to meet your sister." I then explained that
Karen and Palmer were newlyweds and I was really
happy that my older sister had moved back to Virginia
and lived close to me again.

Sergei and I talked non-stop while I drove. The time
flew by so fast it seemed like we were at my sister's
home in no time at all. I found a parking spot in the
crowded lot and we promptly walked toward the stairs
leading to Karen's apartment. Once inside I made the
introductions. Sergei greeted Karen and Palmer warmly
with a friendly handshake and a sincere smile. Their
apartment was small with one bedroom, only slightly
smaller than mine. Unlike my apartment, it was nicely
furnished with a new sofa and loveseat, matching
pillows, curtains and pictures on the walls. It was a cozy
nest for the newlyweds.

Almost immediately Sergei asked if he could look
around their apartment. Because Sergei was new to our
culture I rationalized that it really didn't seem too out of
place. He had asked the exact same question at my
apartment not more than twenty minutes ago. My sister
cheerfully agreed and gave us a quick tour of the place.
I was glad Karen and Palmer were so easy going
because Sergei looked in each and every closet along the
way.

Sergei seemed surprised when we were done with
the tour. "Is that every room? Is that all there is?" he
politely asked. Palmer laughed and assured him that

was everything. Karen and I just smiled at Sergei's slightly inappropriate question. I wasn't sure exactly what Sergei was expecting to see in the apartment but he seemed to be happy with the outcome. We then retreated to the living room where Sergei answered a few questions about life in the United States. After a short visit we said our goodbyes, hugged, and continued on our way. As we walked back to the car Sergei told me he was glad he got to meet my sister and brother-in-law.

When we arrived at the shopping center, Sergei was quick to hop out and run around to open my car door. He had a big smile on his face, gave me a hug, and then threw one arm over my shoulders. He pulled me close to his side as we proceeded to walk through the parking lot. Some guys like to hold hands, some like to link arms when they walk—he liked to casually drape one arm over my shoulders and hold me close, my head almost leaning against his chest and tucked in safely under his arm. Although I didn't feel I needed to be protected in broad daylight in the middle of the parking lot, it was comforting anyway. As we walked, we fell into an easy rhythm as Sergei naturally adjusted his steps to my shorter strides. It felt as if we had known each other for a long time and weren't actually out on a first date.

Our first stop was a popular men's clothing store that I liked to shop at when I needed gifts for my father or brothers. I was sure Sergei would find some fashionable dress shirts there for his meetings. A young male salesclerk was trying to offer help with sizes, and his mouth gaped open when he saw the size of Sergei's chest and shoulders. He wanted to know if Sergei was some sort of famous weight lifter or professional fighter from a foreign country.

The salesclerk found several brands that offered a fuller cut through the shoulders and arms. Sergei and I quickly fell into the ease we found the day before when he tried on coats. As he tried each shirt on, he would come out of the dressing room to model for me, asking for approval and comments. We were like school children again, laughing and cavorting in front of the store mirror. If I pointed out that the sleeves were too tight because his muscles were so huge, he would jokingly flex his arms even more and pose non-stop in the mirror until I couldn't stop laughing. Just like the day before he liked the closeness between us and attention from me. We were both so laid-back in each others' company. It was wonderful to just be ourselves…without a care in the world…or so it seemed. But appearances can be deceiving.

After Sergei purchased two stylish long sleeve shirts we stopped in at a drug store soda fountain for a cold drink and ice cream. I wasn't sure if Sergei had ever been to a soda fountain before. His eyes lit right up when he saw the stools at the counter, and he was very excited to be there. As we sat on the stools, I read the menu to him and explained what some of the items were. He wasn't familiar with all of the names, like the difference between an ice cream float and a sundae. I explained the difference, and for some reason he was fixated on getting a float.

"Yes, ice cream floats, that is what we should have," he said. "We would like to have two ice cream floats," he informed the waitress. "With vanilla ice cream and root beer," he added.

"What if I wanted something else? What if I wanted a chocolate sundae instead?" I mockingly teased him.

"No, this is good, we need to have floats."

"Okay, I guess we will have ice cream floats then!"

When the floats arrived Sergei quickly devoured his while I slowly savored mine, taking my time to reflect on how much fun he was to be with. I alternated between scooping the ice cream out with a spoon and using a straw for the liquid part. I was leaning forward, sipping from my straw when Sergei suddenly grabbed his straw and dunked it into my glass with a playful gleam in his eyes.

"Sergei, what are you doing?" I asked in surprise. Before answering me, he abruptly scooted himself over onto my seat. The two of us could barely fit so he was half sitting, half standing. He wrapped one arm tightly around my waist and held me close so I wouldn't fall off the stool.

"We need to drink like this from same drink, both at same time," he gleefully exclaimed. He leaned over even closer, pressing his face against mine so we were pinned cheek to cheek.

The idea was so funny I couldn't help but laugh and go along with his idea. Besides, I couldn't move if I wanted to. With our faces pressed together, we both sipped on our own straws from my root beer float. He promptly finished first, slurping loudly at the end. *Uh oh, here we go again...creating another scene in a store.* When he was done with the very last sip of my ice cream float, he held me tight a few seconds longer, our cheeks still pressed together, his strong jaw against my soft cheek, our lips almost touching. I was sure a kiss was imminent, and I held my breath slightly in anticipation, enjoying every moment of the closeness between us.

He slowly loosened his arm from my waist and shifted back onto his stool. He then tilted his head forward a little closer to mine as he spoke, "I saw that on TV, the boy and girl shared ice cream float together. They used straws to drink from same glass. I never did that before, I wanted to try like that. You get to hold girl close to you, it is like…how do you say?" He paused as he tried to think of the correct word in English. "It is like sexy."

"Well, yes I guess it is sort of like that," I answered, trying hard to keep from laughing because I couldn't believe he just said that out loud in a public place. I wasn't sure if that was the correct word to use. But then again maybe it was—I could still feel the warm tingling sensation on the side of my face.

On the ride back to my apartment Sergei once again tilted the car seat back. I focused on my driving, but it was hard not to sneak a glance over at him as we spoke. I was surprised to see how incredibly happy he seemed; his smile never left his face. It seemed like we could talk about anything, never running out of things to say. We could just be ourselves with each other, no pretense in the slightest. He began telling me about his life in the Soviet Union, and I found myself mesmerized by his story and even more so by him.

Chapter 9

Sergei's Story

From the book *The Persecutor* by Sergei Kourdakov:
"I took a deep breath, dived, and cut the water perfectly, plunging deep. Then trouble began. Overpowering sensations of shocking cold struck me. The water, when I had tested it earlier, was as cold as any sea I had ever felt. And now that I was immersed in it, my body was shocked by its frigidness. Only one thing filled my mind—get away from the ship."[1]

Fall 1972

I was captivated as I sat next to Sergei on the sofa in my apartment, listening carefully while he continued telling me about his life and subsequently his reasons for defecting from a country that he had loved. Sergei's life was inconceivable to me. It was a miracle that he even survived his escape to freedom. It was a miracle that he was here with me now telling me about his life. What he went through, what he did while in the Soviet Union, was unbelievable and terrifying. I could not imagine that the fun-loving and gentle Sergei that I knew and was falling for could have inflicted terror on Christians who were forbidden to worship in his country. It was chilling to hear, and I wondered if I knew what I was getting myself into.

In my mind, his entire upbringing was heartbreaking. Sergei was born in Novosibirsk in the Soviet Union. He became an orphan when he was four years old. His father was killed while serving in the Soviet Army. Soon after that his mother died, and Sergei was taken in by family friends. The family welcomed him but after a few years their troubled son took his anger out on Sergei.

"The boy put hands on my neck and shoulders. He pushed me under the water in the bathtub. He held me there; he tried to kill me. I thought I was going to die." I was stunned when Sergei put his hands on his throat to demonstrate. For only a fraction of a second I saw the hurt and sadness in Sergei's eyes as he recalled that frightening memory. In that instant I saw the little boy that he was never allowed to be. He quickly pushed those feelings aside and continued talking in his strong, confident manner. "I fought to get away from this boy. I fought him hard. I do not understand why he did this. I was just little boy." Sergei shook his head slowly back and forth, "I think maybe he had problem in his mind." Fearful of eventually being killed by the son, Sergei had no other choice but to run away and try to live on the streets. He was six years old but was determined to survive. It was difficult to hear how Sergei's life had been turned upside down...I felt the pain in his voice.

Sergei was eventually picked up for stealing food and sent to live at one orphanage after another. He learned to take care of himself very quickly. He told me about a caste system at one of the orphanages. If you were at the bottom, you were considered a slave. He eventually fought his way to the top, becoming the king and losing a front tooth in the process. *Self preservation, survival of the fittest,* I thought.

I could tell he wanted me to know all about him, how and why he left the Soviet Union. He wanted to share who he was, drawing me closer to him to know and understand him better. He spoke so matter-of-factly as if to say, this is who I am, accept me for who I am. And I listened without judgment.

After graduating from school he attended a Soviet naval academy. Because of his interest in Communism and strong leadership, he was selected to be a member of the Soviet secret police. As a member of the KGB, one of his duties was to break up secret meetings of Christians or "Believers," as they called them. These meetings were not tolerated because they went against the beliefs of Communism. The Believers were considered dangerous to their government.

He did not go into detail about how they broke up the meetings of the Believers, but he did tell me about one particular young girl named Natasha who changed his life. She was about the same age as he was, and it was very unusual to find young people participating in Christian meetings. He encountered her on three separate raids that he took part in. Even though she had been roughed up by the KGB previously for attending the Christian meetings, she continued to show up knowing that her participation could result in a beating. He could not understand why she came back over and over, why she was not afraid of them, and why she would intentionally endure such suffering.

Natasha told Sergei the reason she was not afraid was because she believed in God. Her profound strength and willingness to be beaten because of her religious beliefs was something he could not understand, and it affected him deeply. Meeting Natasha and trying to understand her undeniable faith in God turned out to be one of the turning points in Sergei's life that convinced him to eventually leave his country.

In the middle of all of this terror, breaking up numerous Believer meetings and secretly reading the confiscated religious material, Sergei miraculously found faith in God. He came to realize that what he was doing was very wrong. The only way for him to pursue religious freedom was to defect from the Soviet Union. He said the KGB was not an organization you could simply walk away from. To be free to follow his desire to know God, to be completely free…he had no other choice but to defect from his own country. It was a risk he knew he had to take.

I sat listening to him, completely spellbound as his eyes stayed focused on mine. A few times I interjected with a comment of total disbelief or to convey my feelings of compassion for the difficult life he suffered. At those times he would reach out and take my hand. He would smile and say that everything was all right. "It is okay, I am okay now, do not have concern for me." He was not looking for sympathy.

He planned his escape carefully. He worked on building up his strength, lifting weights to increase his stamina for the long treacherous swim he knew he would have to make. His opportunity came when he was stationed on a Soviet trawler, a surface ship called the Elagin. He jumped overboard when he was near the coast of Canada and made the treacherous swim toward the lights on the Canadian shore. He barely survived the ordeal and prayed to God, asking for forgiveness, to not let him die when he was so close to freedom.

Sergei was found on the shores of Queen Charlotte Island and was hospitalized for his injuries. After his release he was given a place to live through the kindness of strangers. He learned to speak English during his stay in Canada and became a Christian. In the spring of 1972, less than a year later, Sergei joined Underground Evangelism and moved to California.

The magnitude of what he must have endured overwhelmed me, and I was lost in my own thoughts.

How does one decide to jump off a ship, leave his country behind, and swim toward the unknown? It was clear to me that Sergei was a very smart young man. He was not only street smart, he was book smart—intelligent with a very good head on his shoulders. The combination was powerful, and it made him determined to succeed at whatever came his way. He was not afraid of anything.

As Sergei continued to tell me his story, I was still deeply moved and amazed by his inner strength to change his life. He resolved to dedicate his new life to Christianity and sought forgiveness for those he persecuted. He told me he was writing a book about his changed life and that the book was near completion. "*Sergei,*" was the title of his book. I knew in my heart that he was not the same person he had been in the Soviet Union. It just wasn't possible. The person sitting next to me was completely different.

We stopped at one point to run out for a quick dinner at a nearby restaurant and then returned to my apartment to pick up right where we left off. We talked non-stop until way past midnight, getting to know as much about each other as possible. When it was finally time for Sergei to leave, I called a taxi cab for his return trip to the Christian Fellowship House in Washington DC. He hugged me goodbye and then leaned in close to kiss me gently before he walked out the door. I didn't want him to leave, and I could tell he didn't want to leave either. His sweet kiss still lingered warmly on my lips, a hint of more to come the next time we met. He had only just walked out the door, and I couldn't wait to see him again. He had that sort of effect on me already. I wondered if he felt the same way. I hoped he did—he looked like he did, if his bright smile was any indication.

Chapter 10

Red Roses

Fall 1972

All too soon the weekend was over and I was back in the office on Monday catching up on my work, or at least making an honest attempt trying to. My mind was on overload after everything that Sergei had told me. We had an amazing time together on Saturday and had continued talking for hours back at my apartment. The more we learned about each other, the closer our connection became.

I stopped by Mr. Logie's office to say good morning and check in with him.

"Hello Sam, good morning, how was your weekend? Did you and Sergei have a good time? He told me he had asked you out."

Mr. Logie always had a bright smile on his face, at least when I talked to him. I loved his New Zealand accent, even when he sometimes talked too fast and it was hard to understand what he was saying. At those times, I couldn't help but laugh. It was hard to believe that his former secretaries left in tears. Although, I did hear from other departments that he could be quite forceful and assertive in business meetings. He was tough when he needed to be. It was a good thing we got along so well. I found him to be rather charming and fatherly toward me.

"We had a very nice time together," I said as I gave him a big smile. And I left it at that. I was not in the habit of talking about my dates with my boss. But then again, Mr. Logie was the one who instigated our meeting in the first place, and I could tell he thought very highly of Sergei. Mr. Logie had even offered to drop Sergei off at National Airport (now Ronald Reagan Washington National Airport) later in the day.

I knew I would only get to see Sergei for a short time today before his departure. Sergei told me he had a meeting "out of town" regarding his book but he would be back in DC soon. I didn't even ask where he was flying off to for his meeting. I knew he liked the fact that I never questioned his whereabouts. I understood that there were things…meetings with Government Officials in DC, or parts of his life in the Soviet Union, that he could not share with me. I accepted that part of our time together. I only focused on the part that Sergei would be returning. I couldn't wait to see him again, and I wanted to spend more time with him.

Sergei's schedule was always packed full of speaking engagements and meetings—everywhere. I wasn't surprised though in the least. After what he had shared with me about his new life in the United States, I understood why others were anxious to know all about him. I knew I was going to miss him because I could feel it in my heart, something I didn't quite understand yet.

After lunch Sergei was back in my office saying his goodbyes. He then retreated to Mr. Logie's office to wait for Mr. Logie to make some last minute calls before they took off for the airport. I stopped in briefly and Sergei and I whispered quietly until it was time to leave. Sergei said he had enjoyed our shopping trip and our time together.

"Off we go then," Mr. Logie said as he finished his last phone call. "Sam, I'm dropping Sergei at National Airport. I'll be back soon."

Sergei gave me a long hug goodbye right in front of Mr. Logie. He said he would be returning to Washington DC soon. The look on his face and in his eyes was sincere, and I knew I would see him again. Saying goodbye is the worst; I hated goodbyes, yet there was no way around them and you couldn't escape them. As soon as they left I busied myself with work, trying to concentrate. Work was the best remedy for everything. It kept your mind in check and was professionally rewarding, especially if you enjoyed what you were doing.

In about an hour Mr. Logie returned to the office. He walked in with a huge smile on his face and a dozen beautiful, long-stemmed, deep-red roses. He looked a little awkward as he held them out in front of himself like he wasn't quite sure what to do with them. He was the last person you would ever expect to carry roses around in the office and he did look out of his element.

"Oh, Mr. Logie, you bought roses for your wife!" I exclaimed rather loudly, surprised. "They're beautiful, what's the occasion?" A lot of heads peeked out of office doors, our coworkers had to see this for themselves. My boisterous comments had aroused everyone's curiosity. I'm sure they thought he was in hot water at home and the roses were a truce offering.

"They are not for my wife; they are for you, Sam," he exclaimed. "No, no, they are not from me, they are from Sergei!" he hollered out for everyone to hear. His face turned more than a few shades of red, matching his hair. "The roses are from Sergei!"

I took the roses from Mr. Logie, held them in my arms, and stared at them. I didn't know what to say. They were beautiful, and I couldn't stop smiling. I couldn't believe Sergei wanted me to have roses to remember our time together. It was so soon, no one ever does that. He had only left for the airport a short while ago. We'd only been on one date. It was a charming gesture that I never expected. My heart melted just a little…no, a lot actually. My coworkers stopped by to check out the roses, smiling and commenting, "He sent you roses already," and "Somebody really made a good impression."

Now that Mr. Logie had cleared up who the roses were from he retreated to the sanctity of his office. He wasn't at all in the habit of running errands. After all, he was at the upper level of the Federal Government General Service pay scale at a grade of GS-15, something that Sergei would not have known. That grade was equivalent to a full Colonel if you compared it to the military rankings.

A few minutes later I ducked into Mr. Logie's office to comment on the roses and thank him for the special delivery service. He told me that Sergei was adamant about sending me roses right away; he didn't want to wait. I think he was actually happy to have helped out. I thanked him once more and departed quickly. I was sure he could tell how I felt about Sergei. I could feel the warmth from a blush creeping over my cheeks. *No need to be embarrassed* I told myself. I can't hide my feelings, and Mr. Logie certainly knew how Sergei felt about me. I could only wonder what they talked about in the car ride to the airport.

I dreamily floated on cloud nine that afternoon remembering the shopping trips with Sergei. *How juvenile*, I thought, *I only just met him*. And now I had roses, beautiful long-stemmed red roses to remind me of him. I could hardly wait for the work day to be over; I anticipated a phone call later that evening from Sergei.

At the end of the day, I jumped into my Mustang, which was parked in my reserved spot in the basement garage. Another perk of not working at the Pentagon was that I didn't have to hike in a half-mile or so each morning from the North Parking Lot in all sorts of hideous weather. I placed the roses carefully on the bucket seat next to me where Sergei had been seated only a day ago and exhaled deeply. *Wow*, was all I could think. I drove on autopilot as I made my way home from Rosslyn, taking route 110 towards the Pentagon and then veering off on Columbia Pike, passing the Pentagon on my left and Arlington Cemetery on my right.

I always took a quick look at Arlington Cemetery as I passed by, thinking that if one could choose a final resting spot, I would choose the exact same beautiful section I stared at every day on my way home. Truth really is stranger than fiction. That exact spot I stared at every day would many years later become the final resting place for my beloved mother and father. It was as if all those years of staring at the same location had somehow secretly etched their name into the earth, reserving that section in Arlington Cemetery for them.

I was glad that I lived close to work. Barcroft Apartments were just a short distance away, and I would be home in a few more minutes. At home that evening, with Sergei's roses in a vase, I relived every second of our time together. I placed the roses on the low dresser in my bedroom to the side of the mirror so they reflected two fold in their entire splendor, each red petal tightly clinging to the other, as if holding on for dear life. I sat on the bed and just stared at them; they were beautiful. *Is it possible to like someone that much after only one weekend?* Maybe, but I was extremely practical and cautious and closely guarded my heart. I liked that Sergei was so expressive. We enjoyed being in each other's company. I felt that pull, that unexplained draw toward each other, and I was sure he must have felt it also. There was no denying that sometimes you just know. I was up late since I couldn't fall asleep, and I was still awake when the telephone rang.

"K, sorry it is late, this is Sergei. Did you get the roses?"

"Hi Sergei, I know it's you. I can tell by your accent," I teased him back. "Yes, I did get the roses and they are beautiful. I love them. Thank you for giving them to me."

"I miss you already. That is why I wanted to give you roses," Sergei explained.

"I miss you, too." My heart was beating fast. I was surprised to hear what he was telling me, but I knew from the weekend that he said exactly what he thought at all times.

"I sent you red roses because I miss you very much. I will explain to you. In Russia a red rose is the symbol of a bleeding heart. I miss you and my heart is bleeding now for you. That is why I gave you roses."

I could barely respond. We had only met a few days ago, and yet I knew what he was talking about. My heart ached for him also.

"Sergei, that's beautiful. I love the roses even more now. I miss you, and I can't wait to see you again."

"I will see you soon. I miss you. I have to go now to pick up luggage. Good night," he whispered into the phone.

"Good night," I whispered back as we each hung up.

I fell into a deep sleep dreaming of Sergei and roses and a bleeding heart. This Russian was sweeping me off of my feet. It was a good thing I was already lying down.

Chapter 11

Clean Sweep

Fall 1972

We were on the way back to my apartment in Arlington. Sergei and I had just finished dinner at one of my favorite places, the JW Steakhouse on the top floor of the Key Bridge Marriott. We had an incredible time together, amazing and wonderful and mysterious and startling all at the same time. *I will never forget this night, I will never forget this night* I kept repeating in my mind. The food was great but that wasn't what was so out-of-this-world unforgettable. It was him. It was Sergei. *Did he really kiss me like that? Did he really think I was a spy?* I even started answering my own silent questions. *Yes, he did kiss me like that. Yes, he does think I'm a spy.*

It was hard for me to concentrate on driving with Sergei sitting next to me, especially after the mind-blowing kiss he had just given me at the restaurant. And on top of that I simply could not get his strange comment out of my thoughts. He thought I could be a spy because...I was beautiful! I wasn't sure which was more preposterous, me being a spy or me being beautiful. I thought it was absurd that Sergei thought I was a spy, but I knew he was serious. However, truth be told, I had the same thought about Sergei, that he was a spy. I had even mentioned my concern to Mr. Logie, but he assured me that even though Sergei had worked for the KGB he was not a spy. In fact he laughed at my suspicion and reminded me that Sergei was meeting with Government Officials in the Pentagon. They already knew Sergei visited our office for meetings. "He's been thoroughly checked out—by everyone," he told me. "He's a bona fide defector." I trusted Mr. Logie but still the thought lingered.

When we reached my apartment Sergei jumped out first to open my car door. There was only on-street parking, and I had to park quite far away—a downside to the reasonably priced apartment complex where I lived. I disliked having to walk that far alone at night; there never seemed to be enough lights. But tonight the inadequate lighting was not a concern for me. Sergei pulled me close to him and, with his strong arm draped over my shoulders, I felt protected as we slowly walked up the street.

When I unlocked my front door, Sergei suddenly jumped in front of me and entered first, looking immediately behind the door. As I stepped in, I turned around to lock the door and saw that Sergei was already opening my front hall coat closet.

"Oh, that's the coat closet if you need to hang up your coat," I commented.

"No, I'm just checking," he replied.

I thought he was checking out the apartment layout, maybe looking for the bathroom. He had been to my apartment before, but this time it seemed like he was on a mission. He ran ahead of me and methodically went through every room, looking in every closet, behind each door, even under my bed.

"Sergei, what are you checking for?" I asked. At first I thought it was funny. He moved quickly and efficiently, making a clean sweep of each room with me trailing behind him. When he got to the bathroom, he stopped, suddenly guarded. He paused for a second before he reached up and yanked open the closed shower curtain. I stood there staring at his back, frozen in my tracks, as he stared at the empty bath tub. He had thought someone was hiding in my apartment! This was not a joke to him. I felt a sudden wave of nausea as the reality sunk in. I saw his shoulders slowly relax as he lowered his arms to his side. He turned around to face me.

"I am checking to make sure we are alone," he informed me. And then to justify his strange actions he added offhandedly, "You could be spy."

If no one was there and we were completely alone—was that a good thing or a bad thing? I started to jump to all kinds of conclusions and wondered if it was a wise decision to have invited him into my home. My fears were fleeting though as I looked into his eyes, which were now completely locked onto mine. His eyes were filled with nothing but warmth and compassion.

"Sergei, I'm not a spy. There is no one here in my apartment besides you and me. You know where I work." I tried to assure him, but I didn't know what else I could do to convince him otherwise.

We moved back into the living room and sat on the sofa. He looked relieved after completing his rounds and finding everything in its place. I wondered if he was going to sweep for "bugs" next, just to make sure I didn't have any listening devices hidden around. *This is certainly the most interesting date I have ever had.* I was sure we both could use a drink after that. Between his very public display of affection in the restaurant and then searching for spies in my apartment I knew I definitely wanted a drink. I felt like I was in a James Bond movie. Only I didn't know the script.

"I have bourbon and rum to drink. What would you like?" I asked.

"You don't have vodka? In Russia we like to drink vodka," he said jokingly to me as he leaned back into the sofa to get comfortable.

"No, sorry, I don't have vodka. And you are the only person from the USSR that I know!" I called back as I headed into the kitchen to prepare our drinks. "I will make sure to buy vodka for the next time." I was sure there would be next times—I wanted there to be a lot of next times.

"K, I would like only bourbon in a glass. Please."

I got out my smoke-glazed highball glasses and poured two shots for him. I mixed my one-half shot of bourbon with Pepsi and ice. I was a light-weight when it came to drinking.

We sat close together on the sofa, half turned toward each other as we sipped on our drinks. That comfortable feeling returned, and the strong attraction that was always present was increasing. We talked about anything and everything.

"You still have the roses I sent you," Sergei said, rather surprised.

The roses were in the same vase I had placed them in almost two weeks ago. After they started to drop a few petals I decided to let them dry up to preserve them on their stems with the whole rose intact. They reminded me of him every morning when I woke up. He had spotted them on my dresser when he was in the bedroom looking for...spies.

"Yes, I kept the roses. I think they're still beautiful."

"But they have turned dark, they are ugly."

"No, I think they're really still beautiful. I love them just the way they are. I liked what you told me about how they represent a bleeding heart and you sent them because you missed me."

67

"Yes, I missed you K, it is true," Sergei said. "My heart aches for you and my heart bleeds for you when I am gone."

"I missed you, too." It was all I could manage to say as I smiled at him and stared into his warm eyes. I could hardly believe what he just said to me. He was so honest and open about his feelings. "I really like the Russian belief that red roses symbolize a bleeding heart. It makes the roses even more special," I went on to add. And just like that the conversation changed.

"Why do you live in such a dump?" Sergei asked.

"What do you mean? I think this place is all right." I was surprised and slightly offended by his question. My apartment was clean and neat. I knew I didn't have much, but I was happy with what I did have. Except for the hand-me-down sofa and two table lamps, I had paid for everything myself. I was very proud of that. I had also purchased my car as well. It was a used Mustang, in great shape, fun, and fast when it needed to be. The apartment itself didn't have many conveniences—no air conditioning, and no garbage disposal or dishwasher. The washing machines and dryers were in the basement, but at least they were in the basement of my building. Maybe it wasn't the safest area for a young woman to live, but I was careful.

"A beautiful girl like you should not have to live in a place like this. You should have nice things given to you."

It was such a strange comment; clearly he had a different way of thinking. Maybe he thought all Americans lived a life of luxury. Or else he thought a real spy should be living a life of luxury.

"Sergei, I don't need anyone to give me nice things. I'm very happy with what I have. Besides, who is going to give me things? The only way anyone would give me things would be if I walked the crowded streets of

Washington DC at nights in a tight, sexy, revealing outfit and stood on the corners picking up strange men. Do you understand what I'm saying? I would be a hooker then. Do you understand that word in English?"

"Yes, I understand the word hooker. That is not what I mean. You should not have to live like this. You should have a really nice place to live." He sat still, lost in his thoughts for a moment. "I can give you nice things someday," he said tenderly.

I was surprised by his openness. It was a very heartfelt comment, and I was struck by his genuine feelings that I should be taken care of…that *he* wanted to take care of me. For him to make a statement like that when he left everything in his life behind, when he in essence had nothing, was beyond my comprehension. He was concerned about me, and it touched my soul deeply.

"Sergei, thank you for saying that, but I'm fine. I am really okay. This is a very expensive area to live in and everything costs a lot more here than other places in the United States. I'm used to it." I really never thought about it much before. Actually, I thought I was doing rather well on my own.

Sergei looked at me intently, put his drink down, and pulled me close to him. He put his arms around me and buried his face in my long hair and kissed me gently on the side of my neck as he spoke under his breath. "Beautiful girl like you, you could be spy," he said once more.

I turned and looked into his eyes. I saw confusion, affection, and longing…a reflection of my own eyes. And then it dawned on me. I was a single female alone in my apartment with a very good looking, extremely strong young man, who defected from the Soviet Union, left the KGB, and could possibly be a spy. I should have been frightened, but for some strange reason I wasn't.

Like the moth that is drawn to the flame we were drawn to each other. Unlike the moth though, we knew the outcome could be dangerous. Sergei reached lightly for my chin and turned my head up towards his face and kissed me deeply over and over.

"I am not a spy. I am not a spy. I am not a spy," I softly whispered after each kiss. "You have to believe me," I pleaded.

Chapter 12

A Good Match

From the book *The Persecutor* by Sergei Kourdakov:
"With little hope left, I nevertheless started slowly swimming away from the Elagin. I thought of the documents around my waist. Would someone find them? Would anyone know who I was? Would anyone ever learn the story behind the body they found? My mind became dizzy as thoughts drifted in and out. All my life, from six years of age, I had been alone—no mother or father. It seemed cruel that I would die still alone, lost in a watery grave."[2]

Fall 1972

Sergei planned to stop by on Sunday so we could spend the afternoon together before his flight back to Los Angeles later that evening. Sergei never complained about his demanding schedule and worked everything else around it. He found it exhilarating to talk about his new faith and how it changed him. He was determined to make amends for the suffering he had caused so many people in the Soviet Union.

When the cab dropped him off at my apartment and I opened the door to greet him, he quickly brushed past me and checked every hiding space in my apartment. I trailed behind him in dismay because it broke my heart to watch him. I had the feeling this would be the normal scenario each time he visited my apartment. Once he was satisfied that we were alone, he turned and swept me into his arms, kissing me happily. As he hugged me a small black portfolio slid out from under his arm.

"K, I have something to show you," Sergei blurted out. He could barely contain his excitement.

"What do you have?" I could tell he was very anxious to share the contents with me.

"I have pictures to show you, come sit down, I will show you," he replied as he walked over to the sofa.

He opened the portfolio and pulled out a picture of himself standing in front of a large map of Canada. In the picture he was pointing to the coastline. The look on his face in the picture was ecstatic, one of pure joy.

"When I defected I jumped off the ship and swam toward Canada. I am pointing to the spot where I was found. I did not think I would survive. I prayed to God that I would make it to the shore. I almost died that night."

I leaned over and placed my head on his shoulder. It was impossible for me to imagine what he went through that night when he jumped overboard. He was so young to have made such a life-changing decision to leave his country.

"I'm glad that you are here," I replied softly. I knew why he looked so happy in the photo; he was happy to be alive.

I could tell he didn't want to dwell on that horrible, frightful night near Canada when he fought desperately to keep from drowning. He had more to tell me about the pictures, and his enthusiasm returned immediately. He was eager to share parts of his new life in the United States with me. He then showed me that the portfolio contained dozens of the exact same picture of him. I looked inside and saw handfuls of 8 x 10 glossy, black and white photos, the sort that someone would use for publicity.

"Sergei, why do you have so many copies of the same picture?"

"You would not believe. People ask me all the time for picture. They want me to sign for them. They want my auto..., how do you say that word?"

"Autograph. It's called an autograph when someone asks you to sign a picture for them."

"Yes, they ask for au-to-graph. I think I am maybe like movie star in the United States or something. I cannot believe. Maybe I am famous here. When I tell my story about coming to the United States and how I became Christian a lot of people want to meet me. I do not understand."

He was smiling and laughing when he told me, and it was clear to me that he was amazed by all of the attention he received in this country. I could tell it was important for him to share his story. I knew nothing of his life in Los Angeles and had never even heard of him until I met him in my office. I had no idea of his popularity, that his story was so well known. To him it was only a matter of fact. He was not boasting in the slightest. I knew that he was not trying to impress me. He was telling me the truth, plain and simple. I always considered myself a pretty good judge of character; it was almost as if I had a "sixth sense" in that respect. He was just sharing a part of his life with me. He went on to explain that he spoke at churches and schools and was even on television.

"Sergei, that is wonderful. I'm very happy for you."

He leaned over and kissed me gently. "Here," Sergei said. "Let me sign picture for you. I think you should have picture."

"No, that's all right, I don't need a signed picture of you," I teased him. We were caught up in the moment, and we both started laughing and joking around.

"You do not want picture of me! Why not?" he asked incredulously.

"Sergei, I don't need a signed picture of you because I have you right here with me. I have the real person."

"I will give you one anyway," he chided me.

"Okay, I would love to have your picture. And please write something nice on it," I added sweetly. I could tell that I had unintentionally hurt his feelings. He was laughing as he made a big production of pulling a picture from the portfolio. He asked for a pen and then went to the kitchen table to write me a note on it.

When he returned to the living room he stood in front of me and read his note out loud. "To my dear friend K, with all my Love, Sergei." He smiled as he handed me the photograph, "Here, now you have my picture."

"Thank you, I'm very happy to have your picture. I will treasure it always," I said as I tried to redeem myself from my earlier refusal.

I stood up and hugged him, and we started laughing all over again. I held out the picture and looked at what he had written. I wasn't sure if he just made up something since we were joking about it so much. When I saw his writing on the picture I smiled to myself. I wasn't too sure about the "dear friend" part though. I didn't kiss any of my friends like the way he kissed me, even if they were dear. My eyes lingered over the last part that read "with all my love." Hmmm, I was happy he gave me his picture after all. Maybe that was his intention all along.

He had some other items in the portfolio that were wrapped in clear plastic, and he took them out to show me. We sat back down on the sofa, and he proceeded to tell me about each item. They were his most prized possessions, the documents and photographs he brought from the Soviet Union to prove his story. He told me how he created a waterproof belt to keep everything safe and secure while he swam towards freedom. He handed me each item one at a time and explained what it was. I couldn't believe I was entrusted to hold each treasure. I felt like I was holding his entire life in my hands, and the irony of it all reached deep inside me and touched my soul. He was showing me all that he was, all that he had been, and the bond of our connection tightened again slightly around my heart.

I saw and touched every photo, his birth certificate, and his membership papers for the KGB and the Navy. The photographs were of his friends, his comrades. There were about a dozen photos in all, some from the children's home and the naval academy. Last, but not least, was the photo of Sergei lifting weights to build up his endurance in preparation for his escape. He was not wearing a shirt in the picture and his strength was obvious; he had muscles on top of muscles. *No wonder he can pick me up so easily.* I think I weighed less than those two huge, round weights he was lifting over his shoulders.

He took his time with each photo, explaining the story behind each one. It was his life and he accepted it. When we were finished, he put everything back in the plastic and hugged me. I watched as he carefully wrapped up his former life and placed the small bundle back in his portfolio. He had once again touched something deep inside me. Who Sergei was in the Soviet Union was the person he had to become in order to survive. He was molded to fit into the role that he needed to be at the time. But he had a more sensitive side that no one ever knew about; he had a kind heart. I was able to see that side of him because that was the one thing they could never take away from him. They could never take his heart.

* * *

We didn't have a lot of time left together that afternoon but Sergei remembered that I said I needed to go to the grocery store that weekend because I was practically out of everything. And, for some strange reason, he said he really wanted to help me grocery shop. It seemed like such a mundane thing to do, but he was adamant about going with me.

We grabbed our coats and headed out the door. Before I could close and lock the door, Sergei told me to wait a minute. As we both stood on the landing, he reached into his pocket and pulled out a book of matches.

"What do you need matches for?" I was puzzled.

"I always carry them," he informed me. "Look, I will show you."

He carefully pulled off a good match and then reached up and placed it at the top of the door as he slowly closed the door. He was tall enough to easily place it there so it was barely visible. I could not see it at all.

"This way, we will know if anyone came in while we were gone." He spoke under his breath, "I do this all the time."

I could tell by the look in his eyes that he was serious, and a sense of fear slowly crept over me.

"Who is going to come in, Sergei?" I whispered gravely. "Who?"

"People from my country. They are looking for me," he said firmly.

Then he smiled down at me, threw an arm over my shoulder, and held me close as we walked down the stairs to my car. The pit in my stomach gradually softened, but the idea of Russians breaking into my apartment did not sit well with me at all. But even worse was that Sergei still thought I could be a spy.

I should have known that a trip to the grocery store with Sergei would be anything but mundane. Everything in this country was new to him, and he wanted to experience as much as he could. He had to push the grocery cart, he had to look at everything in the store and ask about all the items. We laughed the entire time and acted like two little kids in a candy store for the first time. I could tell that simply hanging out together, doing something so ordinary, made him feel like he was normal. He could forget about his past life, forget about the danger he felt, at least for just a little while.

When we were done shopping he took a wild ride on the back of the grocery cart in the parking lot as he raced ahead of me to my car. It was quite a spectacle, and I just shook my head in disbelief and smiled. I didn't know a lot about the KGB, but I was pretty sure that wasn't the image they usually projected. As I watched him sailing through the parking lot, I couldn't help but think how free he must have felt. For the first time in his life he was completely free to be himself. And he loved every moment.

I was glad I was part of those special moments and that he felt comfortable enough with me to show me a different side of himself that the rest of the world didn't see. He seemed to sense that I was not the type of girl who needed or wanted to be impressed. In fact I was quite the opposite. I disdained anyone who tried to impress me, and I could spot a phony a mile away.

When we reached my apartment there were no close parking spots, and I had to park a block away. I hated that, especially on grocery day, because it meant I would have to make half a dozen trips to my car to carry everything in and up the stairs. But today there were two of us so it would only mean a couple long treks back and forth from the car to my apartment.

When I started to unload the groceries from the trunk Sergei absolutely would not let me carry one single bag of groceries. Not one. He was going to carry all of them. All at the same time! There must have been about six or seven full brown paper bags, and Sergei insisted that he could carry everything in one trip. He picked up a few bags and then told me to keep handing him the other bags one at a time.

I watched as his huge arms seemed to swallow up one bag after another. It looked impossible to grasp everything, but he managed and made it look easy in the process. I winced as I watched him squeeze and crush everything in his arms. I didn't have the heart to tell him that I knew that the bread, cookies, and crackers would be totally squashed. I was sure the eggs would be broken, too. I was right about all of the above.

The only good news was that when we returned to my apartment the match stick was exactly where he had left it. I breathed a quiet sigh of relief, and Sergei just seemed to take it in stride as he removed the match stick from over my front door. Somehow I knew deep in my heart that he would never let anything happen to me. I trusted him to protect me; I could see it in his eyes when he looked at me. He would always keep me safe.

I insisted that Sergei sit in the living room while I unpacked the groceries so he couldn't see the disastrous results. I smiled to myself as I quickly hid all of the crumbled items in the cupboards and refrigerator. I was smart enough to know that guys will do the strangest things to impress a girl when they really cared about her. I did not want to ruin the moment over a few broken eggs.

All too soon the afternoon ended and Sergei caught a cab to the airport to head back to Los Angeles. He would be returning in a week because he still had business to complete in Washington DC. It was hard to say goodbye again, hard to be apart for even one week. We rarely communicated by phone while he was gone because of the expense. When he knew his next return flight, he would call with details so we could make plans for the following weekend. We both had to watch our budgets carefully since we had limited funds, and lengthy phone calls were not a luxury we could afford.

* * *

I was hard at work in my office on Monday when I was completely surprised by the arrival of another dozen red roses. The attached note read, "My heart is bleeding for you. All My Love, Sergei." My heart skipped a beat and my pulse quickened as I stared at his note and the beautiful roses. A week of waiting to see each other again seemed like an eternity. I missed him so much. I now understood the meaning of a bleeding heart. My heart ached for him...I could actually feel it.

Chapter 13

Embassy Row

Fall 1972

When Sergei returned, I offered to pick him up from the Christian Fellowship House in Washington DC. The expensive cab fare back and forth to my apartment in Arlington was adding up quickly, and I wanted to try and help out a little. The problem was I never drove in DC unless it was a dire emergency, which translated to I didn't know my way around at all. I had only ventured a trip there alone once, maybe twice, before. I dreaded driving there because I was sure I would get lost. And when I get lost I panic. And when I panic all common sense flies out the window. Yes, I dreaded driving there…but the reward would be well worth it. Seeing Sergei was a dire emergency in my mind because I missed him tremendously.

My friends and coworkers knew I never drove in DC, and we often joked about it. They always offered to drive, and I was grateful to them. Mr. Logie knew I would be picking Sergei up after work on Friday and he went over the directions with me several times, assuring me that I would not get lost.

"Sam, it's easy to get there from Rosslyn," Mr. Logie explained. "You just take the Roosevelt Bridge into DC. I know you know where that is! You will swing around the Kennedy Center and it's not much further past that. Sergei is staying in a nice part of town right by Embassy Row. You won't get lost."

I was a clock watcher all day on Friday, and 5:00 couldn't come fast enough. I was really anxious to see Sergei, and my stomach was jumbled in knots. With Mr. Logie's words of encouragement and my resolution to face my fears, I jumped into my Mustang and headed into DC. I was glad there was still a little bit of daylight left as I veered onto the Roosevelt Bridge, over the Potomac River and into the District. Friday traffic was horrible, almost complete gridlock. I was oddly thankful for that though since I didn't know where I was going and it gave me time to read my notes from Mr. Logie and time to find my bearings. I passed the Kennedy Center and then the Watergate buildings. *Not too much further*, I thought. I reminded myself what an amazing, wonderful historic city it really was in an effort to steady my "I am sure I am getting lost" nerves.

Without a single wrong turn or mix up I finally arrived on the right street and was relieved when I was able to find a fairly close parking spot near the Christian Fellowship House. Before I got out of the car I took a minute to check my surroundings. As I sat there, looking up and down the street, I suddenly realized that the sun had set and that it was now totally dark. I had been so concerned about finding my way through the crazy traffic that I totally forgot that it would be nightfall when I arrived. What I thought just a short while ago was an "amazing city" had somehow morphed into a very scary "dark part of the city." For some reason, I have always been afraid of the dark…a carryover from my childhood. I glanced at the secluded sidewalks and streets from my car and didn't see anyone anywhere. There were hardly any cars driving by either. *This is so ridiculous.* With a burst of newfound confidence, I hopped out of the car.

Early winter was definitely in the air, and you could feel the cold blustery winds rolling in from the north. A sudden strong gust of wind whipped my long hair across my face temporarily blinding me. I pulled up my hood to keep my hair out of my eyes as I hugged my wool midi-coat close to me to fend off the evening chill. I quickly looked around again then ran down the street in my high heels, leaping up the steps to the Fellowship House. I didn't care how safe Mr. Logie told me this part of the city was. Walking, or in my case running, down a dark secluded street alone at night in a big city was literally my worst nightmare.

I was slightly out of breath and thankful that the porch light was on. I stood under the covered porch of the Fellowship House feeling a little comforted by the walls that partially shielded me from view. I wasn't really sure what type of place the house was. Was I supposed to walk in and wait in the foyer for someone? I stayed outside and tapped lightly on the door. I waited and waited. After numerous knocks no one came to the door. I was sure I was at the right address. I knocked again, even harder, and still no one appeared. I leaned forward and tried to peer through the window. A lamp was turned on in the foyer, but it didn't help much. It just told me the obvious; there was no sign of anyone at all in the house.

It all seemed very strange, and it was way too quiet, almost eerily quiet. I didn't want to run back down the street to my car alone, but even worse than that was the concern and fear that I couldn't find Sergei. He called earlier in the day to tell me he had arrived at the Christian Fellowship House and would be waiting for me to pick him up. Where was he? For a second I considered trying the doorknob to see if the house was unlocked. If I walked in and encountered a stranger they might think I was breaking in, so I quickly abandoned that idea. I could see *The Washington Post* headlines now with my name in front of the "Arrested for Breaking and Entering" part.

I didn't have a good feeling about any of this. I just wanted to find Sergei. I made one last effort to knock on the door with more force. *Bang, bang, bang*, the noise resounded on the quiet, secluded street. I glanced around furtively, surely someone must have heard that? And then I saw him. Not Sergei. Him! A strange man was glaring at me from the shadows. My loud banging on the door had attracted the attention of a man on the other side of the street. *He wasn't there before, I know that.* I had looked up and down the streets carefully before I got out of my car.

The man was pacing back and forth, staring directly at me. I saw a gun over his shoulder silhouetted in the hazy glow from the street lamp. This was not my imagination. My heart was pounding as I felt fear course through my body. I was sure something awful had happened to Sergei. This would be the perfect spot for something disastrous to take place. It was dark, secluded, and there were no witnesses. No witnesses until I showed up. *Oh my God! Sergei, where are you, where are you?* I ventured a quick glance over my shoulder. The stranger had stopped pacing and was now standing perfectly still as he stared point blank at me. I felt the adrenaline rush as I turned back to the door and started banging repeatedly on the door with my fist as hard as I could, silently praying the man didn't cross the street or come any closer to me. My loud pounding on the door finally worked and Sergei suddenly appeared from inside the house. He practically tore the door off as he opened it and pulled me into his arms.

"K, what is the matter? Why were you banging on the door?"

The words spilled out of me as I frantically held onto him. "There's a man across the street, he has a gun. He followed me and he's been watching me. I didn't know where you were—you didn't answer the door. He has a gun!"

He looked across the street at the man who was standing perfectly still, openly watching our every move. "You are shaking, everything is okay. He is guard from Embassy down the street. I think he heard you making lot of noise and he came to see if you were all right. I was upstairs and could not hear you."

We stood on the porch, Sergei holding me tight in his arms, my head resting on his chest. I was safe with him; I always felt safe with him. I couldn't tell him that when he didn't answer the door I was sure something awful had happened to him. I didn't want him to know his talk about the Russians looking for him had frightened me. I know *he* believed he was being watched by them. I tried to put those fears at rest for his sake, but I failed miserably this time.

My breathing slowly returned to normal in his embrace, and I finally stopped trembling. He gently lifted my face to his and kissed me repeatedly. I returned his kisses with the same urgency and held onto him. Our connection was strong and exhilarating. I was beyond happy that he was all right. I felt all of the tension leave my body as I succumbed to his warm kisses.

"Let's go," Sergei said when we finally broke apart. I reached up with one hand and touched his cheek lightly. Our eyes met and we stood there smiling at each other for a few seconds longer, glad to finally be together again. The porch light cast a dream-like shadow over his face, and I was reminded of how handsome he was. He knew I had been terrified only moments before, and I could see the concern and caring in his eyes. He threw his arm around my shoulders and pulled me close to his side as we took off down the stairs to the sidewalk. Once again I felt safe.

I noticed the Embassy guard had stayed the entire time and had watched everything until we departed. We must have satisfied his concern and curiosity. From our actions it must have been obvious that we were simply a young couple happy to be together again...deliriously happy to be together. My imagination was still on overload though. I felt more like I had just taken part in a clandestine cloak-and-dagger meeting under the dark cover of night with a Russian defector and his mysterious girlfriend—with me playing one of the starring roles.

As we headed toward my car, Sergei politely informed me that he would continue to take a cab; he did not want me to pick him up again. I nodded in agreement as I murmured that I thought that was a good idea. I think I caused enough of a commotion on Embassy Row for one night.

Chapter 14

Hot Pants

Fall 1972

We had a full day of activities scheduled for Saturday, and Sergei and I were both excited about being able to spend so much time together. Before our date, Sergei stopped by to visit the Logie family in Alexandria. I agreed to meet him there afterwards. When Sergei first arrived in Washington DC, he lived with the Logie family for several weeks until other arrangements could be made. They became the family that Sergei never had...they were kind and loving.

Later that afternoon, Sergei and I planned to meet up with my brother and a few of his coworkers for a party. That part was going to be a little tricky to pull off because they all worked for the CIA—something which Sergei did not know.

Saturday was a lot warmer than Friday night had been, and I was pleased because that meant I could wear one of my new outfits to the party. I also wanted to look nice for Sergei. Hot pants had just come into style, and I had recently purchased a two-piece medium blue set with white trim all around. The top had a short skirt attached with an open section in the front to reveal the matching shorts. It was the latest fashion and complemented my figure in all of the right places.

I arrived at the Logie's house a little early so I could visit with everyone before Sergei and I had to leave. When I got out of the car I looked at my clothes and started to feel self conscious about wearing my slightly revealing party outfit in front of my boss and his family. *Too late now, at least everything is covered, and I think my Mom would have approved...well sort of.* It was a good thing I had met Mrs. Logie previously. We had a great rapport and friendship already; she was incredibly warm and friendly. Whenever she called the office we would chat on the phone if I had a little extra time.

Sergei was not shy in the least about hugging me in front of everyone. I could tell he liked my outfit because his arm was permanently around me and he simply could not stop smiling. When I thought about it, he was that way all the time we were together. He always held me close to him in a protective way, not in a possessive way. He was ever the gentleman, kind, attentive, and definitely full of surprises. I never knew when another "as seen on TV" moment might occur. We constantly smiled and laughed—the attraction between us was obvious.

I knew Mrs. Logie was aware of our feelings. She wanted to take pictures of us before we left since we were both dressed up. She thought we looked great together, and I silently agreed with that. Sergei looked especially nice in a tan colored blazer, dark brown and white printed shirt that was casually opened at the collar, and black slacks. Everything emphasized his lean and muscular body.

I already had my camera in my purse to take pictures at the party later, so I handed it to Mrs. Logie as Mr. Logie went to get his own camera. They asked us to pose on the sofa and by the fireplace. As the camera lights flashed back and forth, we just kept smiling at each other. We said they made us feel like movie stars.

When we stood in front of the fireplace Sergei didn't miss a beat; he quickly placed his foot on the raised fireplace hearth and swept me up effortlessly to sit on his leg for the pictures. I was caught off guard, laughing and pleading with him to put me back down. As soon as he lowered me to the floor, I grabbed Sergei and tried in vain to pick him up. Everyone dissolved into laughter, but no one laughed as hard as Sergei. He almost fell over as I managed to scoop up one of his legs and lift it a few inches off the ground. I had never seen him laugh so hard before; he was so happy. After the photography-taking session we said our goodbyes and drove back to my apartment to wait for my brother to pick us up for the party.

Chapter 15

Party with the CIA

Fall 1972

I was surprised that Sergei did not look through every room at my apartment when we arrived, and I quietly rejoiced in that. It was still daylight, and I wondered if that somehow played a part—you can see what you are up against during the day. I kept my fingers crossed that he would enjoy the party later for what it was meant to be, a casual happy gathering of friends.

I never wanted to be dishonest with Sergei, ever, but there was no way around it if he was going to meet my brother. I couldn't tell him that we were going to a party at the home of CIA officers. I felt like he was finally beginning to trust me. If he in any way thought I was delivering him straight into the hands of his former KGB enemy, he would have run as far away from me as possible.

My brother wanted to meet Sergei, and quite frankly, so did his coworkers. I couldn't blame them—how often does one get to meet a defector from the Soviet Union who was a former KGB agent? I knew everyone who was going to be at the party, and I knew Sergei would have a good time, so I agreed to the secrecy part. I knew they wouldn't quiz him. It was simply a social gathering, albeit one where I could not divulge where anyone worked. It had to be that way. This was the only way Sergei could enjoy the evening.

We didn't have long to wait before my brother and his girlfriend arrived. We were all going together since my apartment was on the way, and I certainly had no problem with carpooling after the Embassy Row incident from the night before. I saw Keith's car pull up from the front window of my apartment, and Sergei and I hurried out to meet them. Traffic was unexpectedly light, and we had time to spare, so Keith suggested we stop by one of his favorite bars in DC for a beer before we drove to the party in Maryland. Sergei was pleased to hear that. I think he was a little nervous about meeting my brother. I could understand that; even I thought my brother came across as intimidating sometimes. He was intelligent and very well spoken.

Keith: "We never discussed our occupations outside of our offices and are used to shifting conversation if the subject of work comes up. This usually isn't difficult since other people would usually rather talk about themselves...Sergei wanted to talk about America and all the 'openness' of an open society."

Sergei and I were sitting in the back seat of the car, relaxing and enjoying the ride through the streets of Washington DC as I pointed out the names of the monuments and buildings we passed. Keith was engaging Sergei in conversation, politely asking him about the Soviet Union, where he was born, and general questions. They chatted amicably back and forth until Sergei unexpectedly became extremely uneasy about my brother's familiarity with his former homeland.

"Why do you know so much about the Soviet Union?" Sergei suddenly questioned. He spoke in a low, measured, disquieting voice as his eyes darted around the car at everyone, taking everything in.

This is not going well at all. I turned and looked directly into Sergei's haunted eyes. I felt a cold chill run through me as I tried to comprehend what he must be thinking, that we were taking him somewhere to turn him over to the KGB.

"My brother was a history major in school and knows a lot about foreign countries," I quickly responded, which was the truth. "That's why he knows a lot about your country."

Keith: "My sister had alerted me to Sergei's sensitivity, and he had mentioned that the KGB had contacted him several times since his defection, trying to lure him back. On the other hand I thought Sergei would appreciate a conversation of something familiar, like his hometown, Biysk. Coincidentally, my initial assignment with CIA had been as a photo intelligence analyst…and I specifically worked on Siberia and the industrial and agricultural facilities along the Trans-Siberian Railway, which passes through Novosibirsk just north of Biysk. Also coincidentally, my second assignment was as a Soviet naval intelligence specialist, so I was well informed of Sergei's specifics and had to tread lightly in my conversation. My 'cover story' was that I'd worked with National Geographic magazine, which had done a special on the region. This was true, and I had read the article as part of my own research. Out of college I had also discussed employment with the magazine prior to joining the CIA."

I looked at my brother in the front seat and realized that he could seem a little "shadowy" to someone in

Sergei's position, something I had never thought about before that moment. Keith had deep set, intense blue eyes and an authoritative voice. Our German heritage was quite evident. Even though he was shorter than Sergei, Keith had also done some body-building and power-lifting and had a strong, muscular build. I stole a quick glance at Keith's girlfriend. She gave me a small, concerned smile then turned her gaze back toward the front window as she sat quietly.

Sergei had one arm draped over my shoulders as he kept looking back and forth between me and my brother. I could feel his muscles tensing and his arm felt like a dead weight against my back. I reached for his hand and held it in an effort to distract him. He looked down at our entwined hands and then turned his head to look out of the back window. He slowly slid his body down in the seat and slumped into the corner of the car, out of view from anyone outside.

I leaned toward Sergei and whispered, "Why are you in the corner? What's wrong?" He pulled me over closer to him so that I had to also slide down the seat, and my head rested on his shoulder.

"I think we are being followed," Sergei spoke under his breath. "They are looking for me."

I felt horrible; this couldn't be possible. I quickly sat up and declared with as much confidence as I could, "Sergei, you are all right, nothing is going to happen to you. You are in the United States. Things like that don't happen here. Believe me. You are safe here. We are just going to a party." I wanted to allay his fears of retaliation from the Russians for defecting. I wanted to protect him, and I needed to believe he was safe. My heart already told me that from the very moment that Sergei kissed me in the restaurant, I loved him. It was a secret that I held close, from him, from everyone.

"But first we are stopping for a beer!" I exclaimed to lighten the mood.

That was a good call on my brother's part to stop in for a drink. I saw a huge difference in Sergei's disposition when we arrived at our intended destination...the bar, a real bar! Sergei was once again smiling and carefree as we all looked forward to a pre-party drink.

The bar was quite crowded, which was not totally unexpected for a Saturday happy hour. There were no tables available and no open bar stools either. All of us had to stand as we tried to crowd in around the bar to place our order. It was loud and crazy and fun as we bunched together tightly in our small group. We had to wait a while before our drinks arrived and Sergei, being Sergei, or from the Soviet Union or for whatever rationale, suddenly exclaimed out loud, "Beautiful girl like you should not have to stand."

My cheeks flushed red as the happy hour revelers near us turned to stare at me. They all broke into laughter at Sergei's comment. It had to be his heavy foreign accent and his massive presence because coming from him it was engaging. As soon as those words were out of Sergei's mouth he picked me up and placed me on his leg which was propped up on the bar's foot rail. A young guy that was sitting on the bar stool closest to me swung around and smiled appreciatively when he saw me sitting on Sergei's leg. He quickly got up and offered me his seat. I didn't want to take it, but he politely insisted as he gestured for me to sit down.

As soon as I sat on the bar stool, Sergei leaned over my back and placed his massive arms on each side of me. He gripped the stool with his hands and effortlessly lifted me and the stool up as he casually walked about ten feet away from the bar and the guy who had just relinquished his seat to me. There were cheers from the crowd as his show of strength amazed everyone. When he put me down, he stood next to me and placed his foot up on the lower rung of the stool so that I was as close to him as possible. I was practically sitting between his legs. He made it very clear that I was with him. I was stunned, but it was so funny and outright blatant that I just had to laugh.

As the rest of the laughter in the bar died down, I caught Sergei's gaze and our eyes locked on each other. Even though we were in a crowd of people, I felt an overwhelming sense of intimacy between us, like we were cocooned from the world. It was unexpectedly arousing sitting on the bar stool positioned between his legs like that, and the chemistry between us was palpable. I quickly started talking in an effort to shift the attention elsewhere.

"Sergei, thank you for sending me more roses; they're beautiful. You didn't have to send me more though. I still have the first ones."

"Yes, I know. You should have new ones, so I sent you more. My heart was bleeding for you. I missed you," he replied as he smiled down at me.

Our private moment was broken when Keith and his girlfriend joined us, arriving with beers in hand. They stood next to us, forming a semi-circle around the stool. We raised our beer mugs and laughed as we made a toast. And this was only the pre-party, it was a very good sign of things to come later at the CIA party. I could finally breathe a sigh of relief. I knew the evening would go well, and Sergei would have a good time. After we finished our round of drinks, we headed to Maryland in a more relaxed frame of mind. Any concerns that Sergei had about our true destination had been put to rest.

Keith: "At the bar I got to practice some of my conversational Russian with Sergei. I read a lot of technical documents, but rarely had an opportunity to talk in the language. The conversation was light, mostly about the bar patrons, the friendly atmosphere, his happiness to be in such a setting...although I appreciated from my study that such openness can be frightening to someone unaccustomed, like a long caged animal who, on release, is frightened to be away from protecting walls. I told him a joke in Russian that I remembered and he replied with a humorous take off. I commented on his quickness. He thanked me. We clicked our mugs and drank deep. My sister looked on and asked what we were discussing. Sergei said we were both just being clever."

When we arrived at the party in Riverdale, Maryland we were greeted warmly by our hosts, Jeff and Debbie. Sergei was treated like any other friend, with one special exception though. Sergei was honored with Stolichnaya Vodka shots in a show of camaraderie, something of a tradition among the Soviet analysts in those days. It was the perfect way to welcome him. I skipped the vodka shots and watched quietly from across the kitchen. It was a scene I will never forget and one that Sergei could not entirely appreciate. The significance was not lost on me as I watched Sergei, a former KGB officer, and the other CIA officers toasting in friendship.

My brother raised his glass. *"Na'Zdrovia,"* (to your health) he said.

Sergei broke into a big smile as everyone raised their shot glasses. *"Na'Zdrovia,"* Sergei repeated.

The rest of the evening was perfect. Good fun, good food, good friends and more rounds of vodka shots. Later when we played ping pong, Sergei showed me no mercy. At first he clumsily swung the paddle and missed a few shots, letting me win each game. He was being a gentleman. He did such a good job pretending he didn't know how to play that I actually thought he was horrible at it. It wasn't until I commented that they must not play ping pong in the Soviet Union that he let me have it. He repeatedly slammed the ping pong ball past me and took great delight in watching me chase that little white plastic ball all over the room. Turns out I was wrong, very wrong; they played *a lot* of ping pong in the USSR! And he was really good. He definitely showed me no mercy after my comment. His pride won out over his gentlemanly efforts.

The party was wonderful, and everyone had a great time. True to their CIA-word, the conversation was kept light and it turned out to be the perfect opportunity for Sergei to just be himself and not feel like he was on stage having to relate his life story. My secret mission was accomplished.

> *Keith: "Unaware of Sergei's comfort level, I regularly steered the conversation to future hopes and dreams, a topic Sergei leapt to. He did not talk about his home other than the open skies and beautiful terrain. I didn't press him, which was a good thing. After reading his book I don't believe he had any fond memories of growing up or family or the military. His life was a survival story."*

When the party was over, Keith and his girlfriend dropped us off at my apartment. I noticed when we got out of his car to walk up the sidewalk that Sergei's stride was a little off kilter. He really had a good time at the party, and maybe a little too much Stoli. I teased him about being a little tipsy, and we laughed quietly as we entered my apartment. Sergei still did his walk-through of every room and closet, searched under my bed and last but not least, checked the shower. Then and only then did we go back into the living room and collapse on the sofa. It was late, but we stayed up to talk about the party for quite a while longer. He told me how much he enjoyed meeting my brother and friends.

The soothing effects of the vodka and the late hour finally caught up with Sergei. It was hard for him to even keep his eyes open. He leaned over towards me and rested his head on my shoulder. He was barely awake, but he mumbled slightly to ask me if I would call a cab for him. I reached over and stroked his hair gently off of his forehead, away from his eyes, as I spoke.

"Hey, I'm a little worried about you getting home safely tonight. You can hardly stay awake. I'm even concerned for you to take a cab back into Washington DC."

"No, do not be concerned for me. I will be okay."

But I was concerned for him. He was so tired; he looked like he could drop off into a deep sleep any second. He might not find his way back, even in a cab. I shivered involuntarily thinking about it; I hated the scary dark parts of the city. "Maybe it's better if you stay here for the night. You can stay on the sofa and take a cab back in the morning."

"No, it is okay. I will be okay. I am just tired." He sat up then and looked at me rather sternly. "I can take care of myself; do not be concerned about me."

Somehow I felt that my offer to stay on the sofa sparked something in him, even irritated him a little. He managed a slight smile though as he explained why he needed to leave.

"It is necessary for me to return to the Christian Fellowship House tonight. I am guest. If I do not return they will think something happened to me. I do not want to cause them concern. They are very kind to have me as guest."

"You're right; I understand. They would be concerned if you didn't show up." I reluctantly called a cab. I admired his conviction to be considerate of his hosts. He didn't want to cause them any alarm. It said a lot about his sincerity and his character, and I respected that. And I loved how honest he was about everything. I watched out the window for his cab. When it arrived he sleepily headed toward the door. He turned and kissed me goodbye, throwing his huge arms around me in a tight embrace. His kisses were warm and tender and told me exactly what I already knew. He really didn't want to leave.

Chapter 16

Ya Vas Lyublyu

Fall 1972

And just like that, Sergei was out of my life for a week. He was still in DC, but his busy schedule made it complicated to see each other during the work week. Sergei barely even had time to call me to arrange our weekend dates. The non-communication and separation were difficult, but our reunions were always joyous. We both lived for the weekends when we could be together.

There were times when I thought that Sergei seemed "secretive" about his comings and goings. I remembered Mr. Logie had mentioned the same thing. At first I thought it was because Sergei didn't quite trust anyone. But then I realized he wasn't intentionally being secretive. It was just that it never occurred to him to explain where he was going or where he was staying. He had been alone for most of his life and he never had anyone he really needed to account to outside of work.

For Saturday we planned another date at the Key Bridge Marriott for a night of dancing. They had a live band that performed on the weekends on the top floor of the hotel. We had heard the band play when we were there before, and they were quite good. I was looking forward to going back to the scene of the crime…back to where Sergei stole my heart with his mind-blowing kiss.

Late Saturday afternoon Sergei took a cab to my apartment, and when I opened the door we fell into each other's arms for a brief hug. He immediately did a quick search of my apartment. As soon as he was satisfied we were alone he grabbed me close to him for a proper greeting. We were kissing and talking and hugging all at the same time. He took my breath away; it was wonderful to see him again since our time together was always too short.

After we caught up on each other's week, we left for dinner and dancing. I asked if he wanted to drive my car but he again insisted on me driving as he took the passenger seat. It was only a short ride, but I noticed that Sergei tilted his car seat far back to an almost inclining position.

"Are you tired from all of your meetings?" I asked

"No, I just want to lean back in the car seat."

"If you do that then you will miss the view. I like the tall buildings in Rosslyn; you can see Georgetown, too. I think it's pretty." What he said next would have made me drop dead in my tracks if I wasn't driving a car.

"If I lean back they can't see me. They won't be able to shoot me." His voice was calm and in no way revealed the danger he must have felt.

"Shoot you! No one is going to shoot you, Sergei." My hands gripped the steering wheel tightly as I did my best to keep the car and my alarm under control. I couldn't believe what he said; he couldn't possibly believe that either. "And what about me then? I'm still in plain view; they can still see me. So it's okay for me to get shot but not you? Thanks a lot." I tried to make a joke of it and keep the conversation light-hearted, but inside I was a jumble of nerves.

"They don't want to shoot you. They want me; they don't want you. You are safe." Again his voice was crisp and calm. It was a simple statement of explanation. If it was supposed to make me feel any better it didn't.

I tried to hide my shock as I quickly looked at Sergei, who was stretched out on the bucket seat beside me. *He's serious about this; he's not joking. How can he remain so calm?* At the next few stoplights I did my best to feign disinterest. I twirled a few long strands of my hair in my fingers as I casually looked out the windows at the surrounding cars. I didn't want to look suspicious as I checked out each driver. I sat up straight, in plain view.

I was determined to show I wasn't afraid for Sergei's sake. I was only fooling myself because inside I was trembling. This was clearly taking my fondness for mystery and intrigue to a whole different level. I resolved to be resilient though; I wanted us to enjoy our evening together and try to forget about the rest of the world for a little while longer. My sense of adventure remained strong.

When we reached the parking lot to the Key Bridge Marriott, Sergei jumped out and ran around to my side of the car to help me out. He gently kissed me and pulled me close to his side, his arm thrown over my shoulders as we walked across the parking lot, matching strides as we went. He told me I was safe with him, but I couldn't help wonder if it wasn't the other way around, that he was safe with me.

In spite of the seriousness of our conversation in the car, we did not let that keep us from having a wonderful time. After dinner we joined the party crowd on the dance floor and enjoyed the live band. Sergei was a very good dancer, and it helped us both to unwind. I loved it when they sang a song that you could dance slowly to because we could hold onto each other as we swayed back and forth. I closed my eyes and clung tightly to Sergei as I tried to get lost in the music, lost in his warm embrace, but his words still echoed in my mind...*they want me; they don't want you.*

After a few hours of dancing we were ready to leave. It was too hard to talk with the loud music, and we wanted to have time together to catch up with everything after our week apart. When we reached my apartment, Sergei entered first and checked out all of the hiding places. I accepted that and understood that he felt it was necessary; he wouldn't be able to relax until he completed the inspection. I walked behind him, room after room. When he got to the bathroom and threw back the shower curtain it startled me. It always startled me, and I even knew it was coming. There was never anyone there, but the uncertainty always made me jump. When Sergei was through we headed back to the living room and collapsed on the sofa.

"Would you like a drink? I have a surprise; I bought vodka for you."

"Yes, that is good. I would like some vodka," Sergei said with a big smile on his face.

I fixed the drinks, his vodka straight up and my favorite, bourbon with Pepsi over ice, and then joined him on the sofa. I sat sideways, close to him so we could face each other as we talked. We rarely talked about the Soviet Union or why he defected but tonight was different. I made it a point to never bombard him with questions about his former life. When he had something to share he would always tell me on his own terms, and I would listen intently. He preferred to talk about all of the joys of freedom in the United States and what a wonderful country it was. Tonight he wanted to explain about what he had told me in the car earlier— why he was being followed, why his life was in danger.

He set his drink down on the end table and then motioned for me to do the same. He reached out for my hand and held it while he began to speak in a very serious tone. He looked directly into my eyes as he spoke. He told me that he had been warned previously by some people from the Soviet Union to stop talking about his defection and his religious conversion to Christianity. He said he was being followed and was concerned about that threat. He kept the details to himself. I felt it must have happened again recently.

"K, if something happens to me they will make it look like an accident. I know they are watching me. They are following me. They will make it look like an accident. They know how to do that. Do you understand? They know how to make it look like an accident. Do you understand why I am telling you this?"

"Yes, I understand. But nothing is going to happen to you!" I replied with certainty. He wanted me to know the truth should anything happen to him. If he had any type of accident, it would not be from his own doing. But I didn't want to believe what I was hearing; I didn't want to believe his life was in danger. I was naïve enough to think that things like that could not, would not, happen in the United States. Surely he would be safe and the threats were just that—threats to scare him. Somewhere in the depths of my mind I realized that he was preparing me for something I didn't have the courage to face. Instead I chose to look at the world through rose-colored glasses, a view that things were better than they really were.

Once again I was reminded of his courage and strength. How could he sit there and tell me so calmly that his life had been threatened, that there would be an accident? "Nothing is going to happen to you," I said as convincingly as possible. I leaned over to kiss him, to assure him that I knew he would be all right.

"Even you could be spy." He let out a small sigh as he spoke softly in my ear, hugging me close to his heart.

"I'm not a spy," I whispered back as I tipped my head back to kiss him again.

I leaned back on the sofa and pulled my legs up under me as we continued to talk. I wanted to know more about him, his life that was so opposite of the life I had growing up. My childhood was a happy time, filled with family that loved me unconditionally and happy Christmases and birthdays and picnics in the mountains. I couldn't imagine not having a family and living alone in an orphanage with no one to love me. *You have me to love you, Sergei. You have me.*

When he told me more about living in the orphanage and the fights he had been involved in, I asked him if he had ever been injured. I knew he had a tooth knocked out in a fight, but I didn't know he had been shot and stabbed in other fights. I was shocked to hear that.

"But you are okay now. Where did you get hurt?" I asked. I hadn't seen any signs of injury.

"Come, I will show you," he said as he took my hand and led me to the bedroom. He unbuttoned his dress shirt and loosely folded it, laying it on top of my dresser next to all of the roses. He then pulled off his undershirt and dropped it next to his shirt. I couldn't help staring at his bare chest and the enormous muscles in his arms. I was self-conscious and didn't know what to say.

"Sergei, you really have a lot of muscles; you're very strong." I reached up to his bare arm and tried to put my hands around his bicep but my hands were way too small.

"No, I am not that strong. God is stronger than me," he said.

I was surprised by his answer; I didn't expect him to say that.

"K, let me tell you true story. I will explain."

During one of his last raids with the KGB to break up a Christian meeting of "Believers," Sergei found an elderly woman among the worshipers. He said he raised his arm back to hit her with a special police club that they used during raids. Instead of trying to run or defend herself, the woman continued to pray out loud, asking God to forgive Sergei. She did not pray for herself; she asked for God to forgive Sergei, to help him. She asked God to open his eyes. He could not believe she would pray for him.

"And then the strangest thing happened," Sergei continued with his story. "I could not lower my arm to strike her. Someone was grabbing my arm, holding it back from striking her." As he explained what happened he demonstrated with his own arm. He lifted his left arm up and back behind his head. He made an effort to try to pull his arm forward but kept it behind him in a raised position. "I turned around and there was no one there. There was no one grabbing my arm. K, there was no one there. It had to be God; there was no one else there. It was God holding my arm back so I would not strike the woman."

And I believed him. I would have known if Sergei wasn't honest. I saw the sincerity in his eyes, the incredulous wonder in his own voice. I knew he spoke the truth. I would have been able to tell if he wasn't telling me the truth. I would have seen it in his eyes when he looked at me. I always believed in God, and I knew God worked in mysterious ways and performed miracles.

"Sergei, I believe you. I believe it was God who kept you from hitting the woman."

Sergei was exhilarated…from telling the story and from my believing him. It was hard for me to process everything, the ruthlessness of his past life, and I was bewildered. But I trusted him and accepted that his life had changed. He interrupted my thoughts.

"Here, I will show you where I was wounded." He pointed to a scar over his left breast. "This is small scar from gunshot." And then he lowered his hand to point out a scar slightly above his waist line; it was deeper and the edges were more jagged. "And this is from knife."

He spoke so matter-of-factly, like this was just his normal life in the Soviet Union. My heart ached for him, ached for the horrible life he had, ached for the people he tormented. It was as if I felt his pain, too. I reached up and touched the scar above his breast, then I leaned forward on my tiptoes and gently kissed it. Then I crouched down slightly and kissed the scar by his waist.

"I'm so sorry for you; I'm so sorry," I said as I stood up and looked into his eyes.

"It is okay. I am okay now," he said as he bent over and covered my mouth with his, kissing me tenderly.

Then he unexpectedly picked me up and tossed me gently onto the bed. He climbed over next to me and propped his head up with one arm. We lay there side by side talking and laughing, so comfortable with each other, stopping to kiss between the silences. And when I rested my hand on his chest over his heart, he shuddered ever-so-slightly under my touch and placed his hand on top of mine. We stopped talking, our breathing slowed as we held each other's gaze, and our desire reflected in each other's eyes.

He pulled me closer to him as he rolled over slightly, his weight resting on his forearms. He kissed me passionately, hungrily. It felt like he was holding on to me for dear life. He slowly lowered one arm past my waist to push back my clothing. In doing so he didn't realize that he had shifted all of his weight onto my chest, crushing against me. I could hardly breathe; his shoulder was pressing against my throat.

"Sergei, wait," my voice was barely audible, and I didn't think that he heard me. I desperately needed to tell him something. With his weight on me I was pinned to the bed; I couldn't breathe, and an alarming thought flashed through my mind...it was of a young girl being beaten by the Soviet Police. I took my hands and pushed on his shoulders to try to get his attention. He suddenly shifted his weight and looked into my face with grave concern as I gasped for air.

"K, what is the matter?" he shouted in alarm.

He never realized he had practically smothered me and when I finally caught my breath I called out in dismay, "If you don't stop I'll tell Mr. Logie and he'll send you back to the Soviet Union!" As soon as the words were out of my mouth I wanted to take them back. It had to be the most horrible thing I could have ever said to him. I regretted it immediately. I saw shock on his face; he looked devastated as he leaped off of the bed. He began to pace back and forth in front of my dresser, a look of total despair on his face.

"K, why would you say that to me, why would you say such a thing? I don't understand." He looked visibly wounded. I knew I had hurt him deeply; it was as if I had taken a knife and plunged it into his side. "Do you think I would hit you?"

"No...yes...no, for just a minute I thought that, but no, I know you wouldn't."

"I would never hit you; I would never hurt you. I don't understand."

"I know you would never hit me. That's not why I stopped you." I was trying to put into words what I needed to tell him, but his intense emotional reaction left me reeling.

"Am I not good enough for you?" he cried out in anguish.

"Oh my God, no it isn't that. You are more than good enough for me. It isn't that."

"Then what is it? I don't understand."

I was standing near the bed, unable to even move. I didn't know how to explain why I wanted him to stop. I had been frightened when I couldn't breathe. Telling Sergei he would be sent back to his former country was a terrible thing to say to a man who feared being forcibly returned to the Soviet Union. How I wished I could take those words back.

"I don't know how to tell you so you will understand," I said as I watched him frantically pacing back and forth.

"I don't understand, I don't understand." He stopped abruptly and looked directly at me. "When I was in the KGB I could have any girl I wanted."

His words hit me like a slap in the face. They stung and cut right to my heart...*he could have any girl he wanted.* It was the absolutely worst thing he could have said to me at that moment, and I fought back tears. I was not going to let him see how he hurt me. I raised my hand to my mouth in shock.

"Well, you can't have me," I shot back, my voice trembling.

My response struck him deeply, and he suddenly realized how much he had hurt me. In a quieter tone he continued, "I just don't understand."

He was stunned; he started pacing again with both of his hands along each side of his head. I felt like I was torturing him. He was right; I owed him an explanation. He had read all of my signs right. Every kiss, every touch of mine was filled with love and tenderness. My every response to him, every action said yes. He had crossed the room and was now pacing in front of the closet. I went to him and grabbed him; I wrapped my arms around his waist to make him stop and listen to me. I buried my face in his chest as his arms tenderly encircled me.

"Sergei, I have never been with a man that way before." There, I said it in a way I thought he would understand. With the language barrier I was not sure how to tell him.

"So…you are virgin?"

"Yes, I am. So you understand that word in English?"

"Yes, I understand virgin."

I went on to explain why I blurted out my awful statement. "I would never tell Mr. Logie to send you back to the Soviet Union. I only wanted you to stop so we could talk about this. You couldn't hear me, and I could barely breathe because you fell on top of me." I knew it was only because I felt his crushing weight on me that I had a moment of fear. I trusted him with all of my heart, and I knew he could never raise a hand to me in anger. He was not the same person he had been.

We stood there embracing. He held me close, my cheek resting against his warm bare chest. He gently stroked my long hair with his hand as our fragile heated emotions began to subside. After a few minutes, he lifted my chin upward to gently kiss me. When he finished he held my gaze as he looked down at me; a hint of mischievousness shone in his smile.

"K, do you know what you do to me?"

"No, I don't understand. What do you mean?"

"This is what you do to me." He took my hand and pressed it over the bulging zipper of his trousers, his arousal hard beneath my touch. "This is what you do to me," he repeated.

I didn't know what to say. "I'm…sorry?" was all I could manage. It was such a ridiculous comment that we both looked into each other's eyes and burst into laughter. He pulled on his undershirt and then unceremoniously buttoned his dress shirt, carefully leaving his shirt tail out.

"We need to take things slowly," I shyly said as I tried to think of something to take his mind off of his apparently uncomfortable situation. "I have an idea though." I went to the top drawer of my dresser and pulled out a small box and motioned for him to sit back down on the bed. Sergei looked completely baffled as I opened the box and revealed a deck of cards. I shuffled the cards and taught him a card game.

"Do you have any seven's?" I asked.

"Go Fish," Sergei said as convincingly as possible. He covered his mouth with the fan of cards in his hand as he tried to keep a straight face and keep from laughing.

I looked up and stared right into his beautiful eyes, leering at me suggestively over his mask of cards. Never had the words "Go Fish" been uttered with as much lust behind their meaning as that night.

"This isn't working is it?" I admitted. I grabbed all of the cards and tossed them behind me on the bed. I took his hand and led him to the living room, to the safety of the sofa.

"I think this is better," I said as we both sat down. No sooner did I get the words out of my mouth before Sergei grabbed me and pulled me onto his lap. His kisses were soft and warm on my face, on my neck, my lips. When he was done kissing me, he leaned back, holding my face gently in both of his hands so he could look directly into my eyes.

"K, I love you." He paused for a second and then repeated himself. "I love you," he said tenderly as his eyes soulfully searched my eyes for a response.

I couldn't believe what I was hearing because my heart was beating so loudly at that moment. And with that came the realization that he finally knew I wasn't a spy. I couldn't have been a spy. I didn't seduce him; I didn't sleep with him. After all, everyone knows that no spy in their right mind would ever initiate the "Go Fish" interrogation technique on anyone in favor of having sex. But that was what it took for him to cast aside his doubts.

"I love you too, Sergei." I was delirious with joy. We both were. "How do you say I love you in Russian?" I wanted to be able to tell him in his own language. He went over a few different ways to say it and finally settled on the pronunciation that would be the easiest for me.

"This way is easy for you—Ya vas lyublyu—I love you," he said as he held me tightly in his arms.

It was like a new beginning for both of us. Our world was about to change, and we had each other to hold onto.

"Ya-vas-ly-ub-ly-u," I responded.

"Ya vas lyublyu."

Chapter 17

Man to Man

Fall 1972

I was floating on air when I went to work on Monday. My weekend with Sergei was amazing; we had finally expressed our true feelings. There is nothing more thrilling than young love and acknowledging your love for each other. It's like you've been silently holding your breath and then you can finally let out a huge sigh of relief when you know proof positive that your love is reciprocated. It is simply intoxicating.

When I got to the office I put my coat and purse away, uncovered my typewriter, and prepared myself for the work day. I checked in with my coworkers and then headed down the hall to speak with Mr. Logie to see if he had any special projects lined up for me. I practically glided down the hallway to his office; I held my secret love for Sergei close to my heart. In time I would tell everyone.

"Good morning," Mr. Logie said when I stopped by his office.

"Good morning Mr. Logie. How was your weekend?" I cheerfully asked.

"My weekend was good. I heard you and Sergei had a good weekend also."

"You did?" I was a little perplexed, I wasn't quite sure what he was referring to, how and what he knew about our weekend.

"Yes, well…Sergei needed someone to talk to," Mr. Logie replied.

When he said "needed someone to talk to" I detected a slight catch in his voice. He started shuffling papers around on his desk, turning pages on his calendar. Something was off about his behavior—he didn't look up at me and kept his eyes averted. *He always looks up at me!* As I stared at him, I noticed that his face started flushing bright red. The longer I stood there the deeper his cheeks got, almost matching his bright red hair. I had worked for him long enough to know that he does not embarrass easily. Instantly I knew. I don't know how I knew, but I did.

"Sergei told you!" I exclaimed in shock. I wasn't referring to the "I love you" part of the weekend either.

"Well yes, he did. He needed someone to talk with, so we had a man-to-man talk. He didn't have anyone else to talk to. He didn't understand, and he needed another man to talk things over with."

I wanted to die a thousand deaths right then and there. I could not believe what I was hearing. I could not believe I was having this type of conversation with my boss. My personal life was private. Very private. I didn't even tell my closest friends intimate details about my life. I hadn't even told anyone that Sergei said he loved me.

"Sam, it was simply a man-to-man talk," Mr. Logie replied.

I noticed that his complexion had started to return to normal. I know he hadn't intended to tell me; his crimson color had given him away, and there was no way to gracefully bow out after my direct question. That was it, our conversation was over. With a slight shrug of his shoulders he slid back into his professional mode for which I was thankful.

Men, I don't understand them. I really didn't want to know the details about what they talked about, and I especially did not want to discuss this any further with my boss. I was mortified, plain and simple. I threw myself into my work after that and couldn't wait for the day to end. My feelings teetered from the highs of being in love to the lowest dregs of the earth that my boss knows about my personal love life. I missed Sergei tremendously, but I would have to wait until Friday to talk with him.

I decided that when I got home I would call my mother and tell her about my ridiculously embarrassing situation at work. She was the only one who would understand, and I certainly couldn't tell any of my friends at work. I did not want details of my personal life running the gamut via the office rumor mill. I didn't want anyone to know, period.

My family was in Massachusetts, and I couldn't call that often because of the long distance phone expense. If I did call, the calls were short or my parents would tell me to hang up, and they would call me right back so they would get the bill. Today I didn't care about the money.

"Mom," I hollered into the phone. "I'm so embarrassed. You will not believe what happened at work today! I'm so embarrassed."

"What on earth happened?" my mother quickly asked.

I didn't want her to know all the intimate details about my recent date with Sergei. I just wanted her to know about Sergei's talk with Mr. Logie. In my misery it all came out in one big jumble.

"Sergei and I went out on Saturday and had a great time and later at my apartment when I wouldn't sleep with him he didn't completely understand why and so he told Mr. Logie and they had a man-to-man talk and now Mr. Logie knows that I'm a virgin. Mom, I'm mortified. I'm so embarrassed that my boss knows." As soon as I finished, my mother's very audible sigh of relief could only be summed up as "the sigh heard 'round the world."

"Well, that's not so terrible, is it?" asked my mother.

"Yes, Mom, it's terrible."

"No, it's really not that terrible. Terrible would be if Sergei told him you were easy and that he had sex with you. Then Mr. Logie would think you were the town slut. Now that would be terrible!"

"Thanks Mom, that helps a lot," I facetiously replied.

"Well, I'm right aren't I? It would be much worse for your boss to think you slept with everyone and that you were the town slut instead of the town virgin."

"Ohhh…Mom, it was so embarrassing. I guess when you put it like that it does sound a little funny. For sure, being the town slut is worse when you think about it."

I felt better talking to my mother. We caught up on family news, and I told her more about Sergei. I didn't want to tell her yet that we were in love; I knew she would say it was too soon and I didn't want to get into that. I wanted to wait until after the Christmas holiday. It seemed like a better time, and I would be home and we could talk in person. Besides, she had already expressed her concerns about my dating a Russian defector. I had confided in her previously that Sergei thought he was being followed, though I intentionally omitted the part that his life had been threatened because I didn't want her to worry. During the whole time my mother and I talked on the phone I couldn't help but notice a strange sound, like a muffled click-click sound in the phone.

"Mom, do you hear that strange clicking sound on the phone?" I asked.

"Yes, it's been there the whole time we've been talking."

"It's strange, it's not like static or a bad connection, is it?"

"No, it's different than that."

"Mom, don't laugh, but for some strange reason I think my phone is being tapped. I'm serious."

She didn't laugh. She didn't laugh at all. Her candid response took me by surprise. "I think you're right."

"Yeah, me too," I replied as a queasy feeling started to creep into my stomach. I couldn't believe she thought I was right. I quickly tried to make light of the situation so she wouldn't worry.

"Great, so now my phone is being tapped. So now the entire Soviet Union knows I'm a virgin. And that means the whole world knows I'm a virgin! That's just great."

I was so melodramatic we both broke into laughter as we said our goodbyes and hung up. It did sound ridiculous, but at the same time the idea of my phone being tapped hit me like a ton of bricks. It made sense. Sergei already said he was being watched and that he had been warned. He always checked my apartment each time we entered. He periodically left a hidden match stick over the front door, wedged between the door frame and the door as a warning signal. The idea of my phone being tapped wasn't so farfetched after all.

I was still sitting on my bed after Mom and I finished our phone conversation. *I'm not afraid. I don't really believe any of this*, I told myself. But I needed to check it out, just to satisfy my own curiosity. I made up my mind right then and there to look for a listening device everywhere and anywhere I could think of. I didn't know what to look for but maybe something strange would stand out. *Thank goodness for James Bond movies,* I thought as I planned my room to room search.

I started with the phone still beside me on the bed. It was a beige-colored "Princess" phone—sleek, compact and light weight. When I ordered it from the telephone company, I chose the longest connector cord they offered. That way I could walk around the room with it while I talked. Now, I just stared at the phone as I picked up the handset and studied it. I then carefully unwound the speaker section of the phone until it came off. I didn't know what I was looking for but everything looked like it belonged there. I unwound the hearing section and checked that also. I checked the phone outlet and got a screwdriver to unscrew the plate from the wall. Nothing!

Then I went through every room, looking under tables, feeling with my fingers under the edges of every piece of furniture, every table lamp. I then got out my step ladder and checked out the ceiling light fixtures very carefully. I checked every electric wall socket that I could easily reach. I unfastened the wall plates and looked inside for any unusual objects. I turned up the volume on my stereo and sang as I went about my search as if nothing was wrong. If anyone was listening they could not have known what I was up to. I finished in about an hour and was somewhat relieved that everything appeared normal. *I missed my calling. I really should have been a spy.*

117

Chapter 18

Home for the Holidays

December 1972

When Sergei came over to my apartment on Friday everything seemed different between us. It was even more exciting to be with each other than the time before. This time when we finally got to see each other we fell into each other's arms knowing that our love for each other was reciprocated. There were no doubts for either of us, no more wondering where we stood with each other. He was not shy about telling me he loved me, always in English, and I would respond in Russian, "Ya vas lyublyu."

Since Christmas was only a few weeks away, I asked Sergei if he wanted to meet my parents and spend the holiday with my family in Massachusetts. He was overjoyed and responded quickly.

"K, but of course I want to meet your family. I would very much like to spend Christmas with you."

"I can't wait for you to meet my parents and all my brothers and sisters. I know they will love you, too. I need to check with my parents first to let them know I invited you to join us. I'll call my mom and dad tomorrow and let them know."

My heart surged with joy. We were in love, and Sergei would soon be meeting my family. He didn't pause for even a second when I asked him. I loved that he always spoke so honestly and openly; he did not hold anything back. He was genuinely pleased with my invitation, and I could tell he was as eager to meet my family as I was for them to meet him. I wanted him to join us and see a home that was filled with love and happiness, something I don't think he had remembered in his childhood.

* * *

I called my parents before Sergei came over on Saturday. The news was very upsetting to me. My father was still in the Air Force, and my family was residing on a secure military base. Unfortunately, Sergei would not be allowed admittance onto the base and certainly not into their home. It had nothing to do with my parents not wanting to meet him.

"But Mom, Dad, I want you to meet Sergei. I really want to spend Christmas with him, too. I really like this guy. If he can't come there then I'll make other plans with him to celebrate Christmas elsewhere. I don't think I'll come home for Christmas this year," I informed them adamantly.

"I'm sorry sweetie, it's just not possible for Sergei to come onto the base," Dad said.

"I think you really need to come home for Christmas though," Mom chimed in from the phone extension. "There will be another opportunity for us to meet Sergei. But I really think you need to be here with us this Christmas."

"I'll think about it," was all I could say. "But I'm not very happy Sergei can't join us."

"It's only for a week. You can see Sergei after Christmas can't you?" Mom asked sympathetically. Once again she said, "You really need to be here with your family this Christmas."

"I suppose so; I'll think about it. He really wanted to meet everyone." We said our goodbyes and "I love you's" before we hung up the phone.

I didn't know how I was going to explain this to Sergei. It upset me, and I was sure Sergei would take it the wrong way. I was crushed. My plans, our plans, for spending Christmas week together, going to church on Christmas Eve and sharing all the joy of the holiday season would have to be put on hold for another time. Sergei and I would have to make other plans. I wanted to spend this Christmas with him, and I know he wanted to spend it with me. If it meant not spending Christmas with my family, I was willing to make the sacrifice.

* * *

When Sergei arrived at my apartment on Saturday afternoon I broke the news to him. He said he understood, but I knew he was just as disappointed as I was.

"Sergei, this is terrible. My parents really want to meet you but the base they live on is secure. You understand my father is a Colonel in the United States Air Force. You were a Navy officer; you understand about military life. My dad said he would not be allowed to bring you onto the base."

"K, it is okay, I understand."

"Sergei, I really want us to spend Christmas together. I can change my plans; I don't have to go home. We can plan something together. I would rather be with you."

"You should be with your family. I can make other plans, and we can see each other after Christmas. I can come back after New Year."

"I would rather spend Christmas with you, Sergei."

"I would like to be with you. It is okay. Go and see your family and have Christmas with them. When will you be back?"

"I usually take off the whole week and catch a flight back early on New Year's Eve. Then I have New Year's Day to unpack and grocery shop before I have to return to work. I can come back earlier though."

"No, it is fine. I will make different plans. I wanted to go skiing, so this will be good time for me to plan ski trip. I will come back to see you when you return."

So then it was settled. We would not be spending Christmas together. I still was not happy about the way things turned out with my parents, but Sergei was trying to make the best of the situation. He was very understanding, and he didn't want to keep me away from my family during the holidays. He was ever the gentleman. I, however, felt like I crushed him. The forced smile on his face confirmed it. Neither of us was happy we couldn't be together, but we would make the best of it.

We spent the rest of the afternoon curled up on the sofa talking and trading stories about our lives. Sergei always loved to talk about his life in the United States; everything was new to him. He avoided discussing his life in the Soviet Union. We were comfortable, holding hands and kissing, trying to enjoy every single minute we had. It seemed like no topics were off limits. I asked him something that I was wondering about.

"Sergei, do they really play Russian Roulette in the Soviet Union?"

"Yes, they do," he replied as he looked at me curiously. "It is very dangerous game."

"Have *you* ever played Russian Roulette?"

"Yes. Why are you asking me this question?"

"Because I don't want you to ever do that again, that's why." He looked perplexed and was non-fazed by my comment.

"It is okay, I played Russian Roulette in the USSR when we had a lot of vodka to drink. I was very stupid then. I am not stupid now," he casually replied as he seemingly brushed aside my concern.

I was not satisfied with his answer because he didn't seem to be taking me very seriously. "Sergei, please listen to me, I'm serious. Please don't play that game again."

"Okay."

He still hadn't convinced me so I punched him lightly on his arm with my fist so he would look right at me, see my concern, and know I was serious. "I really mean it, don't play Russian Roulette again," I managed to say as firmly as I could. He grabbed his arm and rubbed it dramatically, pretending I had mortally wounded him.

"Why is this concern?" he asked as he tried to hold back a smile.

"Because I love you, and I don't want anything to happen to you. That's why."

"Okay, I promise. I will never do that again."

He stared at me with a soul-searching glimmer in his eyes. It had suddenly hit him; he got it. He finally understood how much I cared about him. Someone actually cared about him. He pulled me into his arms and smothered me with tender kisses. It had been a long, long time since anyone had ever cared enough about him to be concerned for his safety before. He held me close to him in a warm embrace, my cheek resting over his heart. When I finally leaned back I saw an expression on his face and in his eyes that melted my heart. He knew I loved him and I wanted him to be safe. I was the one person who cared about him just for himself. I wasn't asking anything from him in return, other than his love. From the expression in his eyes, I knew he felt the same way.

Later that evening we had plans to eat at a local Italian restaurant in Arlington. When I pulled my winter coat out of the foyer hall closet, Sergei came over and held it as I slipped my arms into the sleeves. He then retrieved his coat from a chair. As he was putting it on he looked across the room at me and stopped midway with one arm in his coat sleeve.

"You could be wife," Sergei said in the ever-so-direct way he spoke to me. He stood there staring at me with a big smile on his face, his eyes twinkling, his coat slung halfway over his shoulders.

What did he just say? A hundred things ran through my mind. I heard him say that I could be wife. So now he's gone from "you could be spy" to "you could be wife!" Did he mean his wife? Whose wife? Is that a statement or a question? What am I supposed to say back? Was it a proposal? *Good Lord, I don't know how I'm supposed to respond to that.* I really wanted to jump up and down and holler YES but I didn't want to presume he was asking me to marry him. What if that meant something else in the Soviet Union? I needed a Russian translator to tell me what he means in English. I had to say something.

"Ohhh, you think so?" I finally said. I smiled back at him and added, "You could be husband."

It must have been the right answer because he seemed very pleased with my response. He hurried across the room and scooped me up into his arms and gave me a kiss. I wasn't sure if I had just accepted a marriage proposal or not but my answer would have been yes. *Is that how they ask in the Soviet Union?* Either way my answer conveyed I was on the same page as he was. If it wasn't a proposal at least he knew I was open to the idea of marriage. Now it was going to be even harder to be away from each other over the Christmas holiday. We can't possibly be apart; he just said I could be wife. I wanted to tell the world, but I knew I had to wait until we discussed it further. How was I ever going to keep this a secret? I knew everyone would say that it was too soon to be in love, too soon to talk about marriage. But I knew. We both knew.

We walked down the steps of my apartment and out the front door to my car. Sergei threw his arm over my shoulders and held me tightly, shielding me from the cold, dark winter night. It felt right; we felt right together. As we strolled toward my car his words kept echoing in my mind…you could be wife. *Yes, I could.*

* * *

It was Sunday, the last day of the weekend, and our last day together before we went our separate ways for the holidays. Sergei to California and me to Massachusetts. Could we possibly be any further apart at Christmas? It certainly put a damper on the holiday festivities, and we were both feeling a little down in the dumps. Sergei only had a few hours to stop by to visit before he left for the airport to return to Los Angeles. We were trying to squeeze in as much time together as possible.

We were both feeling pretty miserable about the separation over the holidays, but I was trying to be cheerful and make the best of the situation. I suggested a last minute change of plans to cheer us up. I told Sergei I would cancel my plans to spend Christmas with my family so that we could do something together.

We were sitting on the sofa and he had his arms around me as I leaned into him, my back nestled up against his chest. He insisted it was best for me to visit my family, they would want to see me. As we talked I couldn't help but notice how distracted he was; he definitely had something on his mind.

"Hey, are you feeling all right?" I asked. I knew he must be worn out from all of his traveling back and forth across the country, meetings in the Pentagon, and…a busy schedule.

"Yes, I am all right," Sergei answered.

"Are you upset because we won't be able to spend Christmas together? I told you I would change my plans. I can still do that."

"No, it is not that. I am okay."

"Well, you don't seem okay. I think something is bothering you."

"It is nothing. I have something on my mind."

"Sergei, please tell me what's on your mind?" I gently persisted.

"No, it is nothing. I do not want to concern you. Everything is fine."

"Ya vas lyublyu," I said.

"I love you, too," Sergei said as he lifted my chin sideways and leaned over to kiss me.

That was all I needed to hear. He wrapped his arms around me tightly and we held onto each other, savoring the closeness and comfort. I wanted to stay that way forever, close to him, his words from last night playing over and over softly in my mind…you could be wife.

Something definitely was weighing heavily on his mind though. Sergei was trying his best to be his normal cheerful self. He was always so honest and direct with his feelings. Why, I wondered, was he holding something back? What did he not want me to know about? I tried to shake off his troubled mood. He would share his concerns with me when he felt the time was right.

"Hey, I have something for you for Christmas," I said. "I want to give it to you now since we won't see each other until after the holidays."

"K, I did not have time to get you anything. This is terrible. I will bring you a gift from Los Angeles when I come back."

"Sergei, that's okay. I would rather give you my present now. I don't want to wait."

I had gone back to the men's clothing store where we had our first date. I knew they carried shirts that fit his broad shoulders and arms, and I had bought him a shirt he had admired that day. He took the beautifully wrapped Christmas gift and slowly tore the paper away. When he lifted the top of the box off he broke into a big smile. He was very pleased with my selection.

"K, this is very nice, thank you. This is very nice shirt."

"It's one you looked at when we shopped together, do you remember?"

"Yes, I remember," he replied as he unfolded it and held it up to his chest.

I knew he liked it, but I was sure I made him feel bad that he didn't have time to shop while he was in town.

"I still have all my roses from you. I love them," I reminded him. I had dried all two dozen roses and kept them arranged in a vase in my bedroom. They were a constant reminder of him, of our love for each other, and the pain from a bleeding heart when we were apart.

We talked about the holidays. The plan was that I would call him on Christmas day from my parents' home in Massachusetts. The few times that he called me he had to call collect, which he truly disliked. He was staying with a Christian family that was assisting him until he was able to be financially on his own. He was sure that after his book was published he would be in a different situation. I said I would call so that a long distance charge would not be on their phone bill; they had done so much for him already. Sergei gave me the phone number of the family. He and I would have to wait until Christmas day to talk with each other. And when I returned from visiting my family, Sergei said he would call me at my home in Arlington to let me know his travel arrangements back to DC. I would hear from him on New Year's Day.

And then it was time for him to leave. Sergei's cab had arrived. My heart stood still...I didn't want the weekend to ever end. In only a few short hours Sergei would be returning to the West Coast. I had wanted to drive him to the airport, but he politely refused my offer. It was probably just as well, since this was the hardest time we ever had trying to say goodbye. I didn't want him to leave without me, and he did not want to leave either. He gathered his coat and gift and turned to hug me tightly to him. We kissed several times as he tried to head out the door.

"K, my cab is waiting, I have to leave now," he finally said. "I love you."

"Ya vas lyublyu," I replied and released him from my arms. We grabbed one more kiss as he walked out the door.

"Lock the door," he admonished as he waved goodbye.

I closed the door and turned the lock as I listened to his heavy steps fading on the stairs. My heart sank further and further with each step away from me. I couldn't refrain from opening the door back up. I turned the lock and threw the door open.

"Sergei, wait!" I yelled.

"What is the matter?" he called back as he stopped and turned around in surprise. He was halfway down the staircase.

I ran out the door and down the stairs and threw myself into his arms. "Nothing is the matter. I miss you already." I gave him a kiss and then whispered into his ear, "Ya vas lyublyu, Ya vas lyublyu."

I tore myself away and ran quickly back up the stairs. I turned back around when I reached my door and saw Sergei still standing there, watching me with a big smile on his face.

"I love you," he said as he turned and continued down the stairs.

I locked the door behind me and leaned against it. *Yes, I could be wife.* I couldn't stop smiling to myself, and I couldn't wait to see him again. Time stands still when the person you love and care about is on the other side of the country. Time would stand still for me if I couldn't be with the person I loved and he was only on the other side of the street. How was I ever going to make it until after the New Year to see him again?

Chapter 19

Silent Night, Holy Night

December 1972

Christmas in Massachusetts is quite beautiful with all the snow covered pine trees. Christmas with my family is even more beautiful. It was my mother's favorite time of year, and she always started playing Christmas music right after Thanksgiving. Mom and Dad loved having all six children home at the same time. There was always homemade bread and lots of Christmas cookies—tons of Christmas cookies. My favorite Christmas ornament was from my mother. It had a saying on it that read, "All Hearts go Home for Christmas." I loved that saying, but this year my heart was only partly there—the other part was with Sergei.

Even though my parents lived on base, they had a single family house that was quite large. Dad had been promoted to a full Colonel during the war in Vietnam, so his quarters on base were quite nice. Their home was picture-perfect at Christmas time with a big fireplace at one end of the living room and a real Christmas tree to the side of the picture window that overlooked beautiful green pine trees right next to the patio. It made for a cozy holiday, and I knew Sergei would have enjoyed being with all of us. I loved being with all my brothers and sisters, but I had to admit that all I really wanted was to hurry back to Arlington to see Sergei.

At the Christmas Eve church service I even had a hard time paying attention. I kept wishing Sergei and I were together. When we sang *Silent Night, Holy Night* it brought me back to the present. *This is a special night to celebrate the birth of our Lord*, I scolded myself. I quietly prayed for Sergei's safe return, but I couldn't shake the uneasiness I felt. I joined back in singing with everyone, "...all is calm, all is bright." *Yes, all is calm*, I tried to reassure myself.

Christmas morning is total chaos in our house when everyone comes together. We were a family of eight, plus my sister's husband, for a grand total of nine. There is so much noise and laughter and love that it is almost overwhelming, but in the best sense of the meaning.

Everything had settled down by late afternoon on Christmas day. All the gifts had been unwrapped and had somehow disappeared to other parts of the house. It was the calm after the storm of the gift unwrapping frenzy. It was a good time to try to reach Sergei, I thought.

I asked my mother if I could make a long-distance phone call to Sergei in California. She said it was all right, but reminded me to please keep the call short. I knew that wouldn't be a problem because the cost would be on their bill, and I wanted to be considerate of that. Plus I already knew the call would be short because there was literally nowhere in the house to speak privately on the phone. I would have to use the kitchen phone with everyone listening in. *This is going to be the shortest phone call on record.* I couldn't say a whole lot with all the curious ears hovering all around me. I stretched the phone cord around the kitchen corner and dialed the number.

"Hello, is Sergei there?" I asked when the phone was answered by a pleasant sounding gentleman.

"Yes, just a minute," he replied as I heard him call out for Sergei.

"Hello," Sergei said when he picked up the phone. I knew he couldn't talk in private either because I could hear the family he was staying with speaking in the background.

"Hi, Merry Christmas," I cheerfully said.

"Yes K, I knew it was you calling. Merry Christmas," Sergei said warmly.

We kept the conversation light and brief as we talked about Christmas, the cold weather in Massachusetts, and his upcoming ski trip in California. I knew he was even more uncomfortable than I with our lack of privacy on the phone. It was awkward, neither of us could say what we really wanted to say to each other. I told him I needed to hang up soon anyway because my parents were paying for the long distance call.

"Goodbye, I miss you. Ya vas lyublyu," I whispered into the phone. "Have a good time on your ski trip."

"I will call you on New Year's Day, I miss you," he said. "Ya vas lyublyu," he whispered in Russian into the phone.

Because of the lack of privacy he told me he loved me in Russian. That was a first. It sounded beautiful no matter how he said it, in English or in Russian. I hung up the phone and yearned for him more than ever. There was so much I wanted to talk to him about, but it would just have to wait another week. I hated waiting.

Chapter 20

A Bleeding Heart

January 1, 1973

It was great to be home, back in Arlington in my apartment, with my own bedroom, and definitely with my own bathroom and a little more privacy. I had arrived home the day before so I would have time to run to the grocery store, unpack, and catch up on laundry before returning to work.

It had been wonderful to see my parents and siblings. The week actually flew faster than I would have thought as I got caught up in the joys of coming home for Christmas. After all of the happy festivities of Christmas and nine family members converging under one roof it seemed a little too quiet in my apartment, if that was possible.

It was New Year's Day and Sergei would be calling me soon to let me know when he was returning. I could hardly wait to hear his voice again and felt the butterflies in my stomach in anticipation; we would be together soon.

I was unpacking my suitcase around mid-morning when the phone rang. *That's him*, I thought as I eagerly rushed to pick up the phone on my dresser.

"Hellooo," I said in a very cheerful voice.

"Sam, Logie here."

I was really surprised to hear my boss on the other end of the phone. *Why is Mr. Logie calling me at home on New Year's Day? He's never called me at home before.*

"They got him Sam. They got Sergei," he shouted into the phone. I could hear the anger in his voice.

"Where is he, where did they take him?" I was paralyzed with fear. *No, no, no, this can't be happening.*

"Sam, he was shot."

"Oh my God, oh my God. No. Is he all right?" I choked on my own words. I could barely talk as I tried to hold back my tears; a huge lump had immediately swelled up in my throat.

"No, he's not." He paused for what seemed like an eternity. "He's not all right. He's dead, Sergei's dead."

I stood there silently, in shock. It took me a few seconds to comprehend what he told me. And when it did, the sudden jolt of realization hit me like an arrow piercing straight into my heart. My hand flew to my chest, covering my heart to keep it from bursting. My knees started to buckle beneath me, and I leaned forward onto the bed for support so I wouldn't fall on the floor. Somehow I managed to crawl onto the bed as I kept the phone to my ear.

"He's dead, Sergei's dead?" I cried into the phone. I couldn't hold back the tears any longer, I was sobbing.

"Yes, Sergei's dead. I'm sorry, I'm really sorry to have to tell you over the phone. I didn't want to tell you in the office tomorrow. I knew you would want to know as soon as possible. I thought it would be harder for you if you were at work."

"Yes, yes you're right. What happened? Do you know what happened?" I managed to ask between the gasps for air. I could barely think; I could barely breathe. It was difficult to even speak. I needed to know how he died.

133

Mr. Logie tried to calmly explain what little he knew. "He was at the hotel where he was skiing. He was found in his room early this morning with a gunshot wound to his head. They said it was an accident, that he killed himself. I don't believe that though."

There was sadness in his voice, and I knew he was trying to keep his anger under control for my sake. I knew he was hurting, too. Sergei and he had bonded over the last few months; he had become a father figure to Sergei.

"It couldn't have been an accident," I said. "I know it wasn't an accident. He would never have taken his own life. He told me if anything ever happened to him that it would be made to look like an accident." I cried softly into the phone, "Was he alone?"

"Yes, he was alone. Do you have someone you can call to come over?"

"I'll call June; I know she'll come right over. If she's not there I'll ask my sister or brother to come over."

"I'm sorry, I'm really sorry. Are you okay?" Mr. Logie asked.

"Yes, I'll be okay," I managed to say with a hint of truthfulness. "I'll call June right now." I was still crying as I hung up the phone.

But I wasn't okay now. As soon as I put the phone down, hysterical uncontrollable sobs racked my entire body. I curled up on the bed and pulled the bedspread around me. I couldn't stop crying. Somehow I managed to call June and she said she would rush right over; she only lived about fifteen minutes away. She could barely make out what I was saying between all of my anguished cries; she did hear the part that Sergei was dead though.

I grabbed a pillow and pulled it close to me and clung desperately to it. I needed to hold something; I needed to hold him. I needed to feel his arms around me. *He's dead, he's dead, my Sergei's dead. I'll never see him again. The hurt is awful, the pain in my heart is so strong...my heart is bleeding. He was all alone when he died. No one was with him.* And the thought of him dying alone sent me into more uncontrollable sobbing. I wanted to be with him. I thought we would be together. I loved him, and the thought of never seeing him again was unbearable.

When June arrived I somehow managed to pick myself off the bed to answer the door. My body felt heavy and weighted down, and I had to make a conscious effort to even move. June took one look at me, with my face and eyes swollen and tears streaming down my cheeks, and grabbed me and gave me a hug as I cried on her shoulder. She had never seen me so upset; she had never seen me cry over anything. We were so much alike, and June and I were not criers. We never understood why some girls seemingly cried over everything and were so melodramatic. We did not use tears to advance our careers, and we certainly never cried over boyfriend breakups. Today would change all that. Today was different.

"Oh my, you really liked this guy didn't you? I had no idea how much," June said as she tried to comfort me. Her large pretty eyes were overflowing with sympathy.

"Yes, I did, I loved him. Sergei and I were in love," I softly cried out. She knew Sergei and I were dating but so often what happens in the beginning of a new relationship is that friends tend to ignore each other. I had been guilty of doing just that. I had devoted all of my time and attention to Sergei every weekend because of the long distance separations.

"I had no idea," June quietly spoke. "No wonder we haven't gotten together for so long."

"I know, I'm sorry," I replied. "Everything just happened so fast, and Sergei and I wanted to spend as much time together as possible." We sat on the sofa, and I told her everything. I would talk for a while and then the tears would come like an endless flow as June sat there and listened carefully. It was cathartic, in a way, to be able to share such an unbelievable love story. After several hours, when my tears seemed to subside, we reluctantly said our goodbyes.

"Are you going to be okay if I leave?" June asked.

"Yes, I think so. I need to call my parents. I haven't called them yet. I think I can finally talk now without crying every few minutes." We gave each other a big hug, and I slowly walked with her to the door. When she left I closed the door, turned the lock, and put the safety chain in place.

I leaned against the door as I remembered that it was only a short time ago that I ran out that door and down the stairs for one last heartwarming kiss with Sergei. It was the last time he wrapped his loving arms around me in a tender embrace. It was the last time we were able to look into each other's eyes and say "I love you." It was the last time for everything.

Oh Sergei, do you know how much I loved you? Then the heart-wrenching sobs started all over again, gripping my whole body.

I limped over to the sofa. My shoulders were shaking violently, and I curled up in the corner where Sergei used to sit. I cried my heart out that afternoon as the overwhelming grief left my body, washing out in a flood of tears. The tears from a bleeding heart. I remembered that at some point in my hysterical sobbing that I cried out loud in desperation to God, telling him, "This is more than I can bear." I was sure I was going to die from a broken heart. I was alone in my apartment, but I had the distinct feeling of not being alone. The tears suddenly stopped. And just like that it was over. It was as if someone had turned the faucet off, and there were no more tears to shed.

I felt as if Sergei was there with me, consoling me, and I somehow knew that I would be okay, that I would get through this terrible day. I got up from the sofa and went to throw cold water on my face to revive myself. I didn't recognize my reflection in the bathroom mirror. *At least I'm finally done crying*, I thought. The pain was still there, but I somehow had strength to move forward. I called my parents to tell them what happened.

"Hi, Happy New Year," Mom said excitedly when she heard my voice on the other end of the phone.

"Oh Mom, something terrible has happened," I said through choked back tears.

"What happened, are you okay? Were you in an accident?" she said with alarm in her voice.

"Yes, I'm okay. I'm not hurt or anything like that. It's about Sergei."

"Is he okay? What happened?"

"Mom, he's dead. Sergei's dead," I managed to say.

"Oh no," she gasped. "Are you okay? Do you have someone with you?"

"June was here for a few hours; she just left."

"What happened? Do you know what happened? I'm so sorry."

"He was shot with a gun. He was on a ski trip in California, and he was killed at the hotel where he was staying. It happened early this morning. I can't believe it. I loved him. I'm not sure what really happened. Sergei told me he had been warned. It doesn't make sense. None of this makes any sense. It's so horrible, Mom."

"Yes, it is horrible. I'm so sorry. I know you loved him," Mom said. And then in a more somber voice she added, "It's awful, but you know that if you were with him in the hotel room then you could have been seriously injured."

"What?" I asked incredulously. I didn't want to hear that. "You can't be serious?"

"I am serious. That's why I wanted you to come home for Christmas so badly. Dad and I both wanted you home with us. I didn't want you to go on the ski trip with Sergei," she said solemnly.

"Mom, what are you saying?" I was shocked at her certainty.

"I knew you needed to be with us this Christmas. I just had a feeling."

"Oh Mom, if he had stayed here with me in Washington DC he would still be alive. I know he would have been safe with me." I wanted to believe that so desperately. The seeds of guilt were already starting to grow. I felt like it was somehow my fault.

"No honey, it wouldn't have mattered."

I couldn't believe what my own Mother was saying. She was always so practical and down to earth; she was not the type to jump to conclusions. Hearing a statement like that from your own mother has a way of shocking you back to reality. We talked for a while longer and when she was finally sure that I would be all right, we hung up with the promise that I call my sister and brother next.

I made my phone calls to Karen and Keith, and they assured me they were close by if I needed anything at all. They were as shocked as I was. I was drained and didn't want any more company. I finished unpacking and tried to eat a little something for dinner that I was able to scrounge up from the cupboard. Then I showered and washed and set my hair. I purposely left the shower curtain pulled back so it was half open…just in case. Sergei was right; it did make a good hiding place.

I dragged my tired body into my bedroom and fell down on the bed. Sleep evaded me as I tossed and turned. I had so much guilt surrounding his death. What if I had gone skiing with him? What if he had come to Massachusetts with me? What if? What if? Would he still be alive? What if it was my fault?

I stared longingly at the beautiful, dried long-stemmed roses on my dresser, seeking comfort in their promise as Sergei's words came back to me, "I sent you red roses because I miss you very much. I will explain to you. In Russia a red rose is the symbol of a bleeding heart. I miss you and my heart is bleeding now for you. That is why I gave you roses."

He just can't be gone; it must be a mistake. But I knew it wasn't. Finally I fell into a restless sleep with every light on in my apartment. My dreams were filled with loving memories of Sergei mixed in with a haunting fear that somehow it was my fault. His words floated through my mind as if trying to comfort me. "You could be wife. You are safe with me. My heart bleeds for you. I love you."

Later in the night something startled me awake. I sat up abruptly, wondering why all of the lights were still turned on. And then I remembered. As sadness and deep fatigue overcame me I tried to escape the reality of death and collapsed back into my pillow and fought back tears. *What if, what if?* I left all of the lights on. Tonight I did not want to be in the dark.

Chapter 21

A Rose for Sergei

Publisher's note from the book *The Persecutor*:
"On January 1, 1973, he died instantly from a shot from the gun. Though news of his death was first carried internationally as a suicide, this possibility was soon ruled out. An inquest was held and on March 1, 1973, ruled his death to be an accident."[3]

Winter 1973

I don't know how I made it to work the next day, but somehow I managed. Mr. Logie was surprised that I came in at all. He had suggested that I take the day off when we talked yesterday. It was a slight comfort to be around people that knew Sergei, though. Mr. Logie had informed as many of the staff as possible. There were a few who had not gotten the word yet. I put on a stoic face as some coworkers wished me a Happy New Year. In those instances I just smiled faintly back and responded robotically, "Happy New Year." I didn't have the strength to tell anyone what happened. I felt empty inside, cold and hollow.

As the morning passed, I went to a few of my closest friends on other floors in the building to talk with them. Even that was more difficult than I imagined. Not only did I have my own shock and grief to contend with, but I had their shock weighing heavily on me also. By that afternoon, everyone had heard about Sergei's death.

It was difficult for all of us that knew him. It didn't make sense; it wasn't fair that his life was cut short at twenty-one years of age. He had turned his life around and there was so much he wanted to accomplish. He had told me that the final draft of his book was done, and he hoped it would be published soon. His book would explain everything. His new life was dedicated to God, and he sought forgiveness from those he persecuted in the Soviet Union. His life was really just beginning. Our life together was just beginning, and now it was over.

I tried to concentrate on work throughout the day but coworkers would come over to talk with me to offer their condolences. They knew we had dated, and of course, they knew about the roses he sent, but that was the extent of it. They didn't know the real depth of our relationship, that we were in love. Mr. Logie knew though. It was strange beyond belief that my boss knew more about my love life than my best friend June did. He and Sergei had formed a close friendship and the two had bonded in a sort of father/son/man-to-man way, the way that guys do. And he was angry. Mr. Logie was so angry; it was senseless that Sergei died. "Just senseless," he said.

I was surprised later that day when Mr. Logie told me that arrangements were being made for Sergei's funeral service and burial to be held in Washington DC. If Sergei was buried in California I never would have been able to attend the service, and it would have added to the devastation. I needed to see Sergei one last time. I needed to tell him goodbye.

* * *

As it turned out, Mr. and Mrs. Logie would prove to be my salvation over the course of the days that followed. They would be with me every step of the way. I had never been to a funeral before, never been to a viewing, and certainly never to a graveside burial. How fortunate I had been to reach age twenty-one and still have all my family, grandparents, and friends. But now all that was changed and somehow I had to get through the next week, to be there for Sergei. I had heard that funerals were really for the living. But in my mind, it was for Sergei. I needed Sergei to know that he was loved and that he was not alone. I had to do that. And somehow I hoped, by the grace of God, that he would forever know this.

I had decided to wear my black herringbone Chesterfield overcoat for the viewing. I would wear all black for such a solemn day. I purchased a black silk scarf to wrap around my neck from Woodward & Lothrop earlier in the week and was surprised how difficult that was to do.

When I found the right black scarf and held it up to my neck the saleswoman completely startled me with her comment, "A pretty girl like you should not wear black." Her words caught me by surprise, and I stood there dumbfounded. I couldn't believe that she said, "A pretty girl like you." It was such a strange thing to say, and the way she said it haunted me. Why would she say that? Somehow I managed to mumble it was for a funeral, and the woman's kind eyes smiled back knowingly at me. Her choice of words was so peculiar, yet they touched me deeply. It was as if Sergei himself had sent me this message. It sounded so much like something he would have said, a pretty girl like you should not wear black…don't wear black, don't grieve.

On the day of the viewing, I sat in the back seat of Mr. Logie's car as we drove into Washington DC. By

this time I was numb and overwhelmed by sadness. I
didn't even know exactly where Mr. and Mrs. Logie
were taking me. I just let them take the lead, thankful
for all the kindness they showed me. I didn't know what
to expect when we reached our destination. I only knew
that I wanted to be strong for Sergei, to be there for him.

As I quietly sat in the car I glanced down at the
beautiful rose lying across my lap. The rose would be
my last gift to Sergei. My thoughts drifted to earlier in
the day when I walked to the florist across the street
from our office to buy it. Those moments sadly
replayed in my mind…from the sky-walk over Lynn
Street I looked at the Key Bridge Marriott, and the
memories of our kiss in the restaurant were staggering. I
stopped and held onto the railing. *Just breathe, just
breathe,* I told myself. I still couldn't believe that Sergei
was gone forever. With a heavy heart I pulled myself
away from the railing, and slowly made my way to the
next building where the flower shop was located. When
I told the florist I only wanted to buy one red rose, he
wanted me to buy more. He couldn't understand why I
only wanted one rose. *I only have one heart and it is
broken*, I wanted to cry out. "One is all I need," I
managed to tell him. The quiet sadness in my voice said
it all, the tears close but held at bay. Without any
further questions, he went to the display area and
selected a beautiful dark red rose with the petals just
starting to open. It was perfect.

When the car finally stopped, I realized we had
arrived at the Fellowship House. Once we made our
way inside, Mr. Logie asked Mrs. Logie and me to wait
a few minutes while he went to talk with someone. I
held on tightly to the rose clutched in my hand. I had
removed all of the leaves and thorns earlier, carefully
bending each thorn back with my bare fingers, so they
wouldn't pierce into Sergei's skin. I didn't want the

thorns to hurt him. It didn't make any sense, but it was important to me. I leaned on Mrs. Logie physically and mentally for support. I don't know how I could have ever gotten through this without either of them. When Mr. Logie came back he pulled me aside to try to prepare me for what I was about to find out.

"Sam, there is an open casket." Mr. Logie continued in a warm, calm voice, "I don't want you to be shocked when you go into the room and see Sergei's body; he doesn't look like himself. The funeral director said there was a lot of work he had to do because the gun shot was to the head. There was a lot of damage. He tried his best to make Sergei look the same, but it was very difficult."

"Did you see Sergei already?" I asked.

"Yes, I did." Mr. Logie replied.

"Should I see him? Is it okay for me to see him? Is he…all there?" I was afraid to go into the room and look. Afraid I wouldn't be able to keep it together in front of everyone. Afraid I would crumble to the ground and never get up again. Mr. Logie understood what I was asking; I wanted to know *if I* would be okay if I saw Sergei like that.

"You will be able to look at him; he just looks different, so be prepared for that," Mr. Logie said.

We were next in line for the viewing, and Mrs. Logie gently nudged me to go first. I could barely move forward. "You can go alone and say a prayer, stay however long you want," she whispered.

I slowly walked alone into the room toward Sergei's casket, dreading each step that brought me closer to his lifeless body. *I can do this. I have to do this.* And finally I saw Sergei, peacefully at rest, his hands folded at his waist over a Bible. It was him, but the life that was him, was gone.

I reached out and placed one hand on the side of the casket to steady myself. I stared at the form that was him, the heavy thick makeup covering his wounds. The light that always radiated from him was no more. I wanted to hold him one last time. I wanted to kiss him and I wanted to feel the comfort of his arms around me. Instead I silently prayed for him and to him.

Sergei, I am so sorry. I loved you with all of my heart and soul and now you're gone. I'm sorry your life ended when you were so young.

I was trembling inside. It was time. I leaned forward and placed the rose I carried over Sergei's heart. My hand rested gently on his heart with the rose under it. There was no warmth, no life, only the cold hardness of his chest. *This can't be him,* I thought. But it was. With a heavy sigh I continued my prayer.

I brought you a red rose because my heart is bleeding for you. I miss you so much; the pain from a bleeding heart is real. Ya vas lyublyu. I will never forget you.

I touched my fingers to my lips for a last kiss goodbye and then placed my hand on his heart and then to my heart. As I turned to leave it was all I could do to keep from collapsing to the floor as the reality and the accompanying dizziness crept over me. The imaginary rose colored glasses I viewed the world through silently shattered in a million pieces, each razor sharp edge tearing into my bleeding broken heart. The world was suddenly not so perfect anymore.

* * *

I thought I was prepared for the funeral the next day. However, I was not prepared for the emotional toll of a final goodbye. The funeral was on a weekday, so we left work early. Once again Mr. and Mrs. Logie were with me. I sat in the back seat of the Mustang again while Mr. Logie drove into DC. I wondered if they had any idea how much it meant to me to have their support.

I was surprised at how many people there were at the church for the funeral service. It was crowded, and we had to stand the entire time. We were near the back of the church, but I could see that the casket was open again. I could see Sergei, and my heart filled with pain. Even though the church was packed with people, he looked so alone. My heart was breaking for him. They didn't love him like I did. I would not cry though; I had cried enough the day he died.

At one point in the service everyone was given a lighted candle to hold. It was suffocating, the heat from the crowd and the heat from the candles. I couldn't take my coat off, and I thought I would fall over; I was emotionally drained. I barely heard what was said during the service, I missed Sergei so much. When the service was over we went to the grave site, Sergei's final destination.

Everyone was gathered around Sergei's casket at the cemetery and when we arrived we were near the back of the crowd again. We were so far away I couldn't see at all, but I didn't say anything. On impulse, Mr. Logie grabbed hold of Mrs. Logie's arm and my arm and determinedly worked his way to the front of the crowd, pulling us steadily forward. I secretly gave thanks for Mr. Logie's take-charge actions as he boldly pushed past DC dignitaries. He stopped when we were directly along one side of Sergei. We could not get any closer than we were. I could almost reach out and touch

Sergei, the casket was still open. I could see him one last time.

"You need to be right here beside Sergei more than anybody else," Mr. Logie quietly announced.

He could not have been more right. Once again he knew. I stood between Mr. and Mrs. Logie, grateful to have them beside me for support. I felt dizzy; my head was spinning. I was beside myself with grief but did my best to stand on my own, to be there for Sergei. I happened to glance up and noticed that a cameraman was standing back in the distance filming the entire burial service. I was furious that someone was filming such a private moment. *He shouldn't be here.* I wanted him to go away; I glared at the camera in defiance.

As the last rights of the service were read, I lowered my gaze and stared sadly at Sergei. And then it suddenly hit me. The rose was gone! *Where is the rose I gave him?* My words rang out so strongly in my mind that I was sure I had shouted them out loud. I panicked as I felt my pulse quicken; my heart pounded in my chest. It took every ounce of my strength to remain where I was standing because I desperately wanted to leap forward to peer into the confines of the casket, to reach inside and search for his rose. *Where is the rose?* I had to see it. It had to be there. I was angry that the rose had been taken away; I couldn't understand why someone would do that.

My eyes slowly traced over Sergei. And then I saw it. The rose had been moved. Sergei now held my rose in his strong hands that gently rested over the Bible. His hands were folded, a gold cross and chain entwined through his fingers, with my red rose grasped beneath them. The bright crimson color of the rose contrasted starkly against the dark black cover of the Holy Bible. It was mesmerizing, the significance stole my breath as the image was indelibly committed to memory. My rose belonged right in his hands forever, a symbol of my bleeding heart. *He has my rose. He will always know that I love him.* And for the first time in ten days I smiled. I turned to Mrs. Logie and whispered that Sergei was now holding the rose I brought for him. Then I knew it was time for my final goodbye. I pleaded with God as I had an entire conversation with Sergei in my mind.

Dear God, please let Sergei hear me. You have to let him hear me. He has to hear me, he has to. He has to know. Sergei, I will you to hear me. I will you to hear me! I never was a spy. I love you with all of my heart and soul. I will never forget you. You did not die alone; I am here with you. I gave you a red rose to keep with you always because my heart is bleeding for you. Yes, I could be wife. When I said you could be husband I was saying yes to you. Do you understand that? You have to know that my answer was yes. You were more than good enough for me. You have to know this.

It was time to close the casket, and I didn't want them to do that. I was surprised they closed the casket while we were still there. I didn't expect that; I didn't know what to expect. And then the casket started its slow descent into the ground. I stood there like a statue, in shock and disbelief, as I watched Sergei sinking away from me.

They are taking you away from me now and it is unbearable. My heart is bleeding for you. I love you Sergei. Goodbye. I promise I will never forget you. You did not die in vain, your life was important.
Ya vas lyublyu, Ya vas lyublyu.

Chapter 22

Intruders

Winter 1973

At work the next day, Mr. Logie handed me a copy of *The Washington Post.* He told me there was a picture of us in the newspaper that was taken at Sergei's funeral. It was a photo taken from a distance at the grave site. I saw Mr. and Mrs. Logie standing next to a pale, hollow-eyed ghost of a young girl staring blankly at a casket. I barely recognized myself.

Work became my escape. It kept my mind occupied, and I needed that. It helped that I enjoyed working and had a great boss and coworkers surrounding me everywhere. I worked with a new sense of purpose and focus; it helped to numb the pain and sadness in my heart.

The first week after Sergei's funeral was the hardest. It was impossible to accept that he was really gone. I didn't want to accept it; it was too difficult and it hurt. There was a part of me that believed Sergei somehow faked his own death in order to hide from the Russians and that he would secretly come back for me. Every now and then I thought I would catch a glimpse of him in a crowd. But it wasn't him. It was never him.

I sometimes wondered if I was being followed. I tried to put that ridiculous thought out of my mind but I found I looked over my shoulder a little more often, just in case. I still had the unexplained click-click sound in all of my home phone calls though. I refused to be consumed by fear, but it didn't hurt to be a little more cautious.

* * *

I was alone in my apartment on a Sunday evening a few weeks after Sergei's funeral when I heard a faint scratching noise at my front door. *It's just my imagination*, I thought. I tiptoed quietly over to the door and looked out of the small security peephole. I couldn't see anything, but it sounded like someone was trying to open my door. *They must be kneeling on the ground, just out of my view.* I stood motionless, trying to be as still and quiet as possible. Someone was definitely on the other side of the door. In my alarm I bumped the door and jiggled it as I backed away and ran for the phone in my bedroom. *They know I'm here, they know I'm in here! I bumped into the door so they know I'm here and they're still trying to get in.*

I anxiously called my brother. "Please be home, please pick up the phone," I whispered to myself. Keith lived close by, and I knew he could be at my apartment in only a few minutes. I should have called the police but it would have taken forever to explain to the police that I thought someone from the Soviet Union was trying to break into my apartment; they never would have believed me anyway.

It seemed like an eternity but my brother arrived in just a few minutes. I heard a sudden commotion outside my front door. It was over quickly and then Keith knocked on the door and called out to me that everything was okay. I looked through the peephole as a precaution before I opened the door.

"It was them wasn't it? The Russians were trying to break in!" I cried out.

"You were right, there were two of them," Keith told me gravely. "I surprised them when I came in the building and caught them in the act. They took off running; they're gone now."

I could hardly believe it, I was right. They were trying to break in. I stood there in shock and stared at Keith. I didn't know what to do. I was terrified.

"There were two intruders. They had black masks over their eyes, and they had hair all over their bodies. They were horrible looking with all of that hair." He tried to hold back a smile as he continued, "There they were, two cute, furry baby raccoon bandits tearing into the trash bag you left against your door. When I opened the door to your building they scurried past me and ran down to the basement. Someone must have left the door open to the washer rooms down there. I saw the last one's tail disappear into a drain pipe in the basement wall."

I had been scared beyond belief, and my brother stood there smiling and laughing at me. I didn't think it was very funny—it wasn't funny at all. He knew I was scared, and he was making a joke out of it. But maybe that was just what I needed to realize how ridiculous the whole situation was. Too many sleepless nights had taken a toll and my imagination was getting the best of me. I scolded him for teasing me and then we both had a good laugh over me thinking the furry baby raccoons were the Russians. It felt good to laugh though; I actually could laugh again and I was surprised. And I liked it, laughter was much better than the all-consuming sadness I held deep inside my heart.

Shortly after the raccoon incident the strange unexplained clicking sound on my telephone disappeared forever.

Chapter 23

Don't Wear Black

Spring 1973

Spring is my second favorite time of year. The change of season brings with it the promise of bright sunshine and new life with all of the trees and flowers in full bloom. And I appreciated life more this spring than any before. The sadness and grief of losing Sergei was still overwhelming at times. The fact that he had no parents, family, or relatives to care about him was heart-wrenching to me. The fact that he was alone when he died affected me deeply. I felt like I was the only person on the entire planet who truly loved him. He had no one but me. I wondered if my love was enough.

It was a lot to carry in my heart; the pain was still close to the surface. I, however, refused to feel sorry for myself. I was the one that was still living. Sergei left this world tragically at twenty-one and his life was cut short way too soon. He was so close to finding the happiness that he was searching for. I know his life was important and that he tried to make a difference in this world.

I was thankful that I was part of the happiness he knew in the last few months of his life. I decided to focus on the happy memories. Sergei was elated whenever we were together. His smile was constant and contagious; he radiated kindness and warmth. We laughed and talked non-stop, we had that effect on each other. He always wanted to be close to me, our bodies side-by-side when we were walking, always touching. He liked that physical contact, whether it was holding hands, wrapping his arm around my shoulders, or picking me up and placing me near to him. I was always close to him.

I thought about the time he picked me up when I didn't want to step into a mud-filled street in DC. I was going to take a longer way around so my shoes wouldn't be ruined. Without any hesitation he swept me up in his arms and carried me gallantly across the street. He hadn't realized we stopped all traffic because my mini-skirt slid up and exposed my entire back side, revealing my lace bikini briefs to everyone.

I remembered when we shared the seat at the soda fountain and he held on to me tightly so I wouldn't fall off. The times he picked me up to place me on his leg so I wouldn't have to stand, and the incredible kiss in the restaurant that took my breath away. It was as if he had to fit in as much closeness as possible into such a short time…before it all slipped away. He held me, he protected me, he kissed me, and he loved me. Even when he thought I was a spy. And I loved him in return.

There was only one time we were together that I experienced the fear that Sergei must have lived with each day. It was the time my brother drove us to the party at the home of our CIA friends. For just a few minutes in the car that day I felt that Sergei really believed we were turning him back over to the Russians. I saw something in his eyes that I had never seen before. He looked at me with sadness and contempt, his eyes disbelieving and saying everything he could not tell me outright…how could you betray me, how could you deceive me?

It was unimaginable to me that I could pose such a threat, that I could instill fear in Sergei. He was sure we were being followed when we drove through Washington DC to the party in Maryland. I knew that day that he felt the threat to his life was real. Even though I didn't want to accept it at the time, I saw it in his face. I believe that is why every moment we were together was so cherished. There is a part of me that felt he knew his life would be nearing its end soon. As difficult as that was to think about, I truly believe he knew that.

I was surprised I had the strength to move forward without Sergei. I chose to be happy because I knew he would want me to be happy. Maybe it wasn't just a coincidence the day I bought the black silk scarf that the saleswoman in the department store told me, "A pretty girl like you should not wear black." It was as if she was telling me not to grieve.

I had a lot of time to think about Sergei and our chance meeting. In time I came to realize that it probably wasn't by chance after all. We came into each other's life for a reason. I know he wanted to finally live a normal life, to find a wife and have a family. I believe that we were meant to find each other, to love each other for even the limited time we had before he was taken from this world.

It had been five years since Major X imparted his words of wisdom to me when I was only sixteen and working for the Defense Intelligence Agency, "There is not just one person in your life that you will love. There will be several men you will love before you find the one you will marry." And for the second time in my life I wondered how he knew. How was it possible that Major X knew to tell me that? It was a total mystery, but I found solace in his words. His words held the promise of a new life, a new love still to come.

Chapter 24

Summer of Change

Summer 1973

Part of moving forward was trying to venture into the dating world again. My heart was not in it, but I knew I had to make the effort. Devoting all my energy to working at the office wasn't the answer. The few times I did go on dates they bordered on disastrous because, in the back of my mind, I knew that it was too soon. Sergei was still so close to my heart.

I also knew when it was time to let go. On a warm summer Saturday afternoon I carefully took the two dozen red roses off my dresser. With a sad heart I gently wrapped the beautiful dried flowers in white tissue paper and placed them in a container. All the memories were safely tucked away. The sudden ache in my chest caught me by surprise, the pain from a bleeding heart. *Sergei, I have to take the roses away; I have to let go. I have to.*

It was to be the summer of change. Whether I wanted it or was ready for it, change found me anyway. One bright sunny day I decided to leave work right at 5:00 p.m. I usually waited for the work day to be over before I started clearing my desk and work space to close down for the day. The blue skies and sunshine beckoned me to leave work right on time. I said goodnight and headed out of the office first.

It was unusual to find the elevators completely vacant of any office workers, but I was a little ahead of my normal schedule. I reached the basement parking garage, stepped out, and rounded the bank of elevators. My car was parked in the far corner of the building in my reserved parking space. It was a great parking spot along the wall; no one parked close to me, and I liked that my car doors never got hit.

It was strange that the entire basement garage was secluded that evening. As I cleared the elevators I caught a sudden flash of movement out of the corner of my right eye, and I felt the chill of an ominous presence. I swung around instantly as a man stepped out of the dark from behind the bank of elevators. I stopped dead in my tracks.

I boldly stood my ground and didn't run. There was no one else around. There was nowhere to run. As the man came into full view beneath the overhead lighting I saw that he was young, about my age. He told me he wanted to get in the car with me and go someplace. I was relieved that he didn't have a Russian accent, which was a totally crazy thought in that situation. There was no way he was getting in the car with me.

I remembered my mother's frightening words of caution, "You can fight and die outside of your car, or you can let an attacker in your car and he will drive you to a secluded place, rape you first, and then kill you anyway!" Mom had an overprotective way of scaring you senseless sometimes, but her words rang true. I would rather fight. Physically I was no match for him, I was small in comparison, but I confronted him as I shouted back.

"What? You want to get in my car? Of course you can't get in my car! What's the matter with you? I'm not taking you anywhere! Are you crazy?" I shouted all at once.

I continued my tirade, staring directly into his eyes, until he slowly backed away and disappeared through the door into the bank of elevators. When I was certain he was gone, I turned and bolted fifteen feet or more to my car. I could barely put the key into the lock I was shaking so badly. In the face of certain danger I didn't know how I was able to confront him like I did. I was sure that the fact that I still "looked over my shoulder" from time to time left me in a more cautiously prepared state of mind.

The next day when I told my coworkers about the garage incident they all suggested I change my parking spot. Mr. Logie insisted I go immediately to the parking garage management office in our building and demand a safer parking spot. The would-be-attacker now knew where I parked in the basement of our building.

The parking office assistant was completely understanding of my situation. It didn't hurt that she was a young female. She parked in the same building, and it could have been her the man approached. She was glued to her seat as I retold the disturbing details. She admitted she would not have been able to confront the stranger, and she was shocked to hear that I had. She was visibly shaken and realized the urgency.

I was instantly assigned to an above-ground parking spot in the Lynn Building, which was right next to ours. The two office buildings shared a large connected underground parking garage, but the Lynn Building also had a few above-ground parking spots. I could park above ground and walk outside to my office building next door without ever having to walk through a basement garage again. I was very fortunate to snag such a prime, safe location.

After I signed the papers I went right away to move my car to the next building. I was not waiting until the end of the day. I quickly found my new reserved parking spot; it was right next to a bright shiny red Pontiac Lemans. I was glad to be parking above ground and more than happy to put the attacker scare out of my mind.

* * *

Around the beginning of August I heard there was a job opening for an Administrative Assistant in another division of the Office of the Secretary of Defense. The job was in the building next door, the Lynn Building, the very building where I now parked my car. It would mean a very nice promotion for me if I landed the job, but I was hesitant to apply. If there was any way I could stay where I was and be promoted then I could continue working in a job that I really loved and I could also continue working for Mr. Logie. It would be the best of both worlds. I talked with Mr. Logie about the possibility of a promotion and he promised to check into it; he did not want me to leave either.

As fate or destiny would have it, it was not possible for my job to be raised to a higher paying GS-scale position. With Mr. Logie's blessing, I applied for the new position right before the job announcement closed. I told myself it was a step in the right direction as I sought to advance higher within the Federal Government. The new promotion would take me out of the secretarial field and into administration where the salary scale was higher. It was a difficult step because I was reluctant to make any changes. I still felt comforted surrounded by those who remembered and knew Sergei.

Soon after I applied for the new job I received a call to schedule an appointment for an interview. It turned out that I had the very last appointment on the final day of the interviews. At the end of the interview I was told that the job was mine if I wanted it.   I accepted immediately.

My new boss then informed me that the only difficulty, strange as it seemed, would be finding a place to park in the Rosslyn area. He knew there were no longer any parking spots available for our office. He was shocked when I told him I currently had a parking spot right in the garage of his office building, the Lynn Building. *What a strange coincidence,* I thought.

"Well then, it was meant to be," he said. "Congratulations, when can you start?"

* * *

It all happened so quickly. I couldn't believe I got the job and the big promotion that went along with it. *Change is good,* I told myself. Even though I knew it would be hard to leave a job that I really liked, and most of all Mr. Logie, the boss that everyone wishes they had just once in their lifetime. I gave my two weeks notice with regrets.

And just like that I was leaving an office where such an important chapter in my life had played out. I met Sergei right after I turned twenty-one, and I couldn't believe that a year had passed. In some ways it felt like I had lived a lifetime already. I learned many of life's lessons way before anyone that young needed to.   I understood that some people are not meant to be in your life forever.

When Sergei and I first met he said I should have nice things given to me. *He* wanted to give me nice things. He only knew he gave me beautiful red roses…a symbol of his bleeding heart because he missed me when we were apart. Sergei would never know about his other gifts. He gave me kindness and truth. He gave me strength that I never thought was possible.   He taught me to be open and honest about my true feelings for another person, to say the words that need to be said. He taught me to find happiness each day—you might not have a tomorrow.

Knowing Sergei had changed me. I knew the relationship that Sergei and I shared would shape the course of events to forever come my way. I missed Sergei deeply, but the happy memories would stay. The memories of our time together would be safeguarded in my heart forever.

Epilogue

Fall 1973

I started my new job in September, my favorite time of year, and only a few days shy of my twenty-second birthday. The first day of a new job is always overwhelming. I was fortunate, however, to be in a division with a group of exceptionally nice people, and I felt welcomed and at home right from the start. Everyone was quite friendly, which is always a concern when you leave a job and people you really liked.

My second day on the job brought a very pleasant, unexpected surprise. It turned out that the owner of the shiny red Pontiac Lemans worked in my immediate office. He was fairly new, about my same age, and I discovered that I would be working with him. *What a coincidence, I park right next to him in the garage.* He was very good looking, had an easy, friendly smile, and carried himself with confidence—what I would normally think of as the intelligent, sexy, quiet type. When he found out my birthday was in a few days he asked me out right on the spot to celebrate. I couldn't believe it when he leaned over my desk when no one else was around and quietly asked me to go out with him. It was totally out of the blue, and he caught me off guard. I did like how straightforward he was though, and my cheeks flushed slightly as he waited for a reply.

* * *

And somewhere between teaching me how to ski and play tennis that year…he also taught me how to love again.

A year and a half later I married that cute guy who drove the shiny red Pontiac Lemans. On our wedding day I carried a beautiful cascading bouquet of white and green carnations, my favorite flower.

Author's Note

Summer 2014

Writing a book was something I never planned to do. But time has a way of changing our thinking and circumstances led me to understand that it was the right thing to do. The controversy surrounding Sergei's life, even after all these years, has weighed heavily on me. It is my hope that by telling this story that some understanding of the person Sergei had become will shed some light on his miraculous life. He was a completely changed person from the man he was in the Soviet Union.

I wrote *A Rose for Sergei* from the perspective I had when I was twenty-one years old. The book is based on the memories that stand out the most in my mind. It wasn't until I finished writing that I saw all the pieces of the puzzle fall into place. There were several coincidences that surprised me and they definitely gave me cause to wonder. Was it really just a coincidence that I met Sergei? Or was I meant to come into his life at exactly that time? Did Major X have amazing insight; did he somehow know I was going to play a part in Sergei's life...or that Sergei would play an important role in my life?

The freedom Sergei so desperately sought, the freedom he hoped for when he defected from the USSR, was elusive. He wanted to live his life to the fullest. I believe that during the time I knew Sergei, he did know happiness. He confidently spoke about his newfound

163

faith in churches.   He was anxiously anticipating the release of his book.   And he found love.

Only in death, was he free indeed.

Addendum

When I was notified of Sergei Kourdakov's death, the details of how/what actually happened were not immediately known. I believed Sergei was alone when he died, and that is how I portrayed this event in my book. I never questioned it, and honestly, I really didn't want to know the tragic details.

It would be many years before I discovered the investigation into Sergei Kourdakov's death revealed that he *was not* alone when he died—he was with a skiing companion. Newspapers reported that a gun loaned to Sergei accidentally fired while he was handling it. The bullet struck Sergei in the head, killing him instantly.

The results of the investigation do not affect my story because *A Rose for Sergei* was written from what I knew at that time.

Acknowledgments

Thank you:

To Suzanna Pangilinan. You were right! The perfect place to begin writing this book was with "Sergei's kiss." Thank you for everything. You are a true friend.

To Mr. Kirk H. Logie, Sr. and his family. Our shared memories of Sergei connected us in many ways.

To my brother Keith Kenny for his invaluable writing contributions.

To my sisters Karen Robeson and Kelly Simonsen— my first supporters and first readers. Thank you for editing suggestions and for validating my writing.

And most importantly, thank you to my husband and family for all their love and support.

About the Author

The daughter of a U.S. Air Force pilot and stay-at-home mother, K. Kidd grew up living in Okinawa and all across the United States. She was seventeen when she started working for the Federal Government in Washington DC. The mystery and intrigue of the intelligence world fascinated her.

After leaving Government service, K. Kidd worked as an administrative assistant for Fairfax County Public Schools in Northern Virginia. She currently resides in Virginia with her husband and family.

To this day she still looks behind the shower curtain.

* * *

Thank you for reading A Rose for Sergei.

Blog & Photographs
ARoseforSergei.blogspot.com

Twitter @KKiddAuthor

Facebook & Goodreads
K. Kidd Author

Pinterest.com/ARoseforSergei

Contact K. Kidd
ARoseforSergei@gmail.com

References

[1]Kourdakov, Sergei (1973). *The Persecutor*. Fleming H. Revell Company. p.16

[2]Kourdakov, Sergei (1973). *The Persecutor*. Fleming H. Revell Company. p.19

[3]Kourdakov, Sergei (1973). *The Persecutor*. Fleming H. Revell Company. Publisher's Note. p.254

Made in the USA
Middletown, DE
10 January 2020